D0477705

Dictionary
of
English Grammar

This edition published 1995 by Brockhampton Press, a member of
Hodder Headline PLC.

ISBN 1 86019 013 8

Printed and bound in Slovenia

Contents

A

a *see* **indefinite article**.

a-, an- is a prefix derived from Greek, meaning 'not', 'without'. Older words using it include agnostic, anarchy, anonymous. Several modern words have been formed using it, as in apolitical, asexual, atypical.

abbreviations are shortened forms of words usually used as a space-saving technique and becoming increasingly common in modern usage. They cause problems with regard to punctuation. The common question asked is whether the letters of an abbreviation should be separated by full stops. In modern usage the tendency is to omit full stops from abbreviations. This is most true of abbreviations involving initial capital letters, as in TUC, BBC, EEC and USA. In such cases full stops should definitely not be used if one or some of the initial letters do not belong to a full word. Thus television is abbreviated to TV and educationally subnormal to ESN.

There are usually no full stops in abbreviations involving the first and last letters of a word (contractions) Dr, Mr, Rd, St, but this is a matter of taste.

Abbreviations involving the first few letters of a word, as in 'Prof' (Professor) are the most likely to have full stops, as in 'Feb.' (February) but again this is now a matter of taste.

These are mostly formed by adding lower-case *s*, as in Drs, JPs, TVs. Note the absence of apostrophes. *See also* ACRONYMS.

ablative refers to a case in Latin grammar that expressed 'by, with or from'. In English this case does not exist, prepositional phrases being used its place.

-able is a suffix meaning 'that can be', as in laughable, readable, washable. *See* **adjective**.

abstract noun is a noun which is the name of a thing that cannot be touched but refers to a quality, concept or idea. Examples of abstract nouns include 'anger', 'beauty', 'courage', 'Christianity', 'danger', 'fear', 'greed', 'hospitality', 'ignorance', 'jealousy', 'kudos', 'loyalty', 'Marxism', 'need', 'obstinacy', 'pain', 'quality', 'resistance', 'safety', 'truth', 'unworthiness', 'vanity', 'wisdom', 'xenophobia', 'youth', 'zeal'. *See also* CONCRETE NOUN.

accent commonly refers to a regional or individual way of speaking or pronouncing words, as in 'a Glasgow accent'. The word is also used to mean emphasis as in 'In hotel the accent is on the second syllable of the word' or 'In fashion this year the accent is on longer skirts'.

Accent also refers to certain symbols used on some foreign words adopted into English. In modern usage, which has a tendency to punctuate less than formerly was the case, accents are frequently omitted. For example an actor's part in a play is now usually spelt role but originally it was spelt rôle, the accent on *o* being called a circumflex. The accent is most likely to be retained if it affects the pronunciation. Thus cliché and divorcé usually retain the acute accent, as it is called, on the *e*. On the other hand, the accent known as the cedilla is frequently omitted from beneath the *c* in words such as façade/facade, although it is there to indicate that the *c* is soft, pronounced like an *s*, rather than a hard sound, pronounced like a *k*. The grave accent is retained in English in some words and phrases derived from French, as *mise en scène*.

accusative refers to a case in Latin grammar, the equivalent of 'objective'. It is sometimes used in English instead of 'objective'.

acronyms, like some **abbreviations**, are formed from the initial letters of several words. Unlike abbreviations, however, **acronyms** are pronounced as words rather than as just a series of letters. For example, OPEC (Organization of Petroleum Producing Countries) is pronounced o-pek and is thus an acronym, unlike USA (United States of America) which is pronounced as a series of letters and not as a word (oo-sa or yoo-sa) and is thus an abbreviation.

Acronyms are written without full stops, as in UNESCO (United Nations Educational, Scientific and Cultural Organization). Mostly **acronyms** are written in capital letters, as in NASA (National Aeronautics and Space Administration). However, very common **acronyms**, such as Aids (Acquired Immune Deficiency Syndrome), are written with just an initial capital, the rest of the letters being lower case.

Acronyms which refer to a piece of scientific or technical equipment are written like ordinary words in lower-case letters as laser (light amplification by simulated emission of radiation.

active voice is one of two voices that verbs are divided into, the other being PASSIVE VOICE. In verbs in the active voice, commonly called *active verbs*, the subject of the verb performs the action described by the verb. Thus, in the sentence 'The boy threw the ball', 'throw' is in the active voice since the subject of the verb (the boy) is doing the throwing. Similarly, in the sentence 'Her mother was driving the car', 'driving' is in the active voice since it is the subject of the sentence (her mother) that is doing the driving. Similarly, in the sentence 'We saw the cows in the field', 'saw' is the active voice since it is the subject of the sentence (we) that is doing the seeing. *See also* PASSIVE VOICE.

acute accent refers to a mark placed over some letters in certain languages, such as French, to indicate vowel length, vowel quality, pronunciation, etc. It is found in English in some words that have been borrowed from the French, as in 'fiancé' and 'divorcé' to indicate pronunciation.

-ade is a suffix meaning 'fruit drink', as in 'lemonade', 'orangeade'.

adjectival clause is a kind of subordinate clause which describes or modifies a noun or pronoun. *See under* RELATIVE CLAUSE, the name by which it is better known.

adjective is a word that describes or gives information about a noun or pronoun. It is said to qualify a noun or pronoun since it limits the word it describes in some way, by making it more specific. Thus, adding the adjective

'red' to 'book' limits 'book', since it means we can forget
about books of any other colour. Similarly, adding 'large'
to 'book' limits it, since it means we can forget about
books of any other size.

Adjectives tell us something about the colour, size,
number, quality, or classification of a noun or pronoun, as
in 'purple curtains', 'jet-black hair', 'bluish eyes'; 'tiny
baby', 'large houses', 'biggish gardens', 'massive es-
tates'; five children', 'twenty questions', 'seventy-five
books'; 'sad people', 'joyful occasions', 'delicious food',
'civil engineering', 'nuclear physics', 'modern languages', 'Elizabethan drama'.

Several adjectives may modify one noun or pronoun, as
in 'the small, black cat', 'an enormous, red-brick, Victorian house'. The order in which they appear is flexible and
can vary according to the emphasis one wishes to place on
the various adjectives. However, a common sequence is
size, quality, colour and classification, as in 'a small,
beautiful, pink wild rose' and 'a large, ugly, grey office
building'.

Adjectives do not change their form. They remain the
same whether the noun to which they refer is singular or
plural, or masculine or feminine.

All the above examples of adjectives come before the
noun, but not all adjectives do so. For information on the
position of adjectives *see* ATTRIBUTIVE ADJECTIVE, PREDICA-
TIVE ADJECTIVE, POST-MODIFIER.

Many **adjectives** are formed from either the past participles of verbs, and so end in -*ed*, or from the present participles and so end in -*ing*. Examples of adjectives ending

in *-ed* include 'annoyed', 'blackened', 'coloured', 'damaged', 'escaped', 'fallen', 'guarded', 'heated', 'identified', 'jailed', 'knotted', 'labelled', 'mixed', 'numbered', 'opened', 'pleated', 'recorded', 'satisfied', 'taped', 'used', 'varied', 'walled', 'zoned'. Examples of adjectives ending in *-ing* include 'amusing', 'boring', 'captivating', 'demanding', 'enchanting', 'fading', 'grating', 'horrifying', 'identifying', 'jarring', 'kneeling', 'labouring', 'manufacturing', 'nursing', 'operating', 'parting', 'quivering', 'racing', 'satisfying', 'telling', 'undermining', 'worrying', 'yielding'.

Several **adjectives** end in *-ical* and are formed by adding *-al* to certain nouns ending in *-ic*. Examples include 'arithmetical', 'comical', 'critical', 'cynical', 'fanatical', 'logical', 'magical', 'musical', 'mystical' and 'sceptical'. Sometimes the adjectives ending in *-ical* are formed from nouns that end in *-ics*. These include 'acoustical', 'ethical', 'hysterical', 'statistical' and 'tropical'. Several adjectives end in *-ic* and are formed from nouns ending in *-ics*. These include 'acoustic', 'acrobatic', 'aerobic', 'athletic', 'economic', 'electronic', 'genetic', 'gymnastic', 'histrionic' and 'linguistic'.

Other common adjectival endings include *-ful*, as in 'beautiful', 'dreadful', 'eventful', 'graceful', 'hateful', 'tearful' and 'youthful'. They also include *-less*, as in 'clueless', 'graceless', 'hatless', 'meaningless' and 'sunless'.

Many adjectives end in *-able* and many end in *-ible*. There are often spelling problems with such adjectives. The following adjectives are likely to be misspelt:

Some adjectives in *-able*:

abominable	disreputable	nameable
acceptable	durable	non-flammable
adaptable	durable	objectionable
adorable	enviable	operable
advisable	excitable	palpable
agreeable	excusable	pleasurable
amiable	expendable	preferable
approachable	foreseeable	readable
available	forgettable	recognizable
bearable	forgivable	regrettable
bearable	healable	renewable
beatable	hearable	reputable
believable	immovable	sizeable
blameable	impassable	stoppable
calculable	impeccable	tenable
capable	implacable	tolerable
changeable	impracticable	transferable
comfortable	impressionable	understandable
commendable	indescribable	unmistakable
conceivable	indispensable	usable
definable	inimitable	variable
delectable	insufferable	viable
demonstrable	lamentable	washable
dependable	manageable	wearable
desirable	measurable	winnable
discreditable	memorable	workable

Some adjectives ending in *-ible*:

accessible	divisible	perceptible
admissible	edible	permissible
audible	exhaustible	possible
collapsible	expressible	repressible
combustible	fallible	reproducible
compatible	feasible	resistible
comprehensible	flexible	responsible
contemptible	forcible	reversible
credible	gullible	risible
defensible	indelible	sensible
destructible	intelligible	susceptible
digestible	irascible	tangible
discernible	negligible	visible

See also COMPARISON OF ADJECTIVES, COMPOUNDS, DEMON-STRATIVE ADJECTIVE, DETERMINER, INTERROGATIVE ADJECTIVE and POSSESSIVE ADJECTIVE.

adverb is a word that adds to our information about a verb, as in 'work rapidly'; about an adjective, as in 'an extremely beautiful young woman'; or about another adverb, as in 'sleeping very soundly'. **Adverbs** are said to modify the words to which they apply since they limit the words in some way and make them more specific. Thus, adding 'slowly' to 'walk', as in 'They walked slowly down the hill', limits the verb 'walk' since all other forms of 'walk', such as 'quickly', 'lazily', etc, have been discarded.

There are several different kinds of **adverbs**, categorized according to the information they provide about the word they modify. They include adverbs of time, adverbs of place, adverbs of manner, adverbs of degree, adverbs of frequency, adverbs of probability, adverbs of duration, and interrogative adverbs.

Adverbs of time tell us when something happened and include such words as 'now', 'then', 'later', 'soon', 'afterwards', 'yesterday', etc, as in 'He is due to arrive now', I will call you later', 'She had a rest and went out afterwards', 'They left yesterday'.

Adverbs of place tell us where something happened and include such words as 'there', 'here', 'somewhere', 'anywhere', 'thereabouts', 'abroad', 'outdoors', 'overhead', 'underground', 'hither and thither', etc, as in 'I haven't been there', 'They couldn't see her anywhere', 'His family live abroad', and 'We heard a noise overhead'.

Adverbs of manner tell us how something happens and include a wide range of possibilities. Frequently adverbs in this category are formed by adding -*ly* to an adjective. Examples of these include:

adjective	*adverb*	*adjective*	*adverb*
anxious	anxiously	mean	meanly
bad	badly	narrow	narrowly
cautious	cautiously	pale	palely
dumb	dumbly	quick	quickly
elegant	elegantly	soothing	soothingly
fearless	fearlessly	tough	toughly
hot	hotly	unwilling	unwillingly
interested	interestedly	vain	vainly
joking	jokingly	weak	weakly
lame	lamely		

Some adjectives have to be modified in some way before the suffix -*ly* is added to form the adverbs. For example, in adjectives ending in -*y*, the *y* changes to *i* before -*ly* is added. Examples of these include:

adjective	adverb	adjective	adverb
angry	angrily	happy	happily
busy	busily	merry	merrily
canny	cannily	pretty	prettily
dry	drily	silly	sillily
easy	easily	tatty	tattily
funny	funnily	weary	wearily

Note the exceptions 'shyly', 'slyly', 'wryly'.
Adjectives ending in -*e* frequently drop the *e* before adding -*ly*. Examples of these include:

adjective	adverb	adjective	adverb
able	ably	peaceable	peaceably
feeble	feebly	true	truly
gentle	gently	unintelligible	unintelligibly

Suffixes other than -*ly* that may be added to adjectives to form **adverbs of manner** include -*wards*, as in 'backwards', 'heavenwards'; -*ways*, as in 'edgeways', 'sideways'; -*wise*, as in 'clockwise', 'moneywise'.

Some **adverbs of manner** may take the same form as the adjectives to which they correspond. These include 'fast', 'hard', 'solo', 'straight', 'wrong', as in 'She took the wrong book' and 'Don't get me wrong'.

Adverbs of degree tells us the degree, extent or intensity of something that happens and include 'hugely', 'immensely', 'moderately', 'adequately', 'greatly', 'strongly', 'tremendously', 'profoundly', 'totally', 'entirely', 'perfectly', 'partially', 'practically', 'virtually', 'almost', as in 'They enjoyed the show hugely', 'The office was not adequately equipped', 'We strongly disapprove of such behaviour', 'He was totally unaware of the facts', 'They are virtually penniless'.

Adverbs of frequency are used to tell us how often something happens and include 'never', 'rarely', 'seldom', 'infrequently', 'occasionally', 'periodically', 'intermittently', 'sometimes', 'often', 'frequently', 'regularly', 'normally', 'always', 'constantly', 'continually', as in 'She never eats breakfast', 'We go to the cinema occasionally', 'He goes to the dentist regularly', 'Normally they travel by bus', 'He is in pain constantly'.

Adverbs of probability tells us how often something happens and include 'probably', 'possibly', 'conceivably', 'perhaps', 'maybe', 'presumably', 'hopefully', 'definitely', 'certainly', 'indubitably', 'doubtless', as in 'You will probably see them there', 'He may conceivably pass the exam this time', 'Presumably they know that she is leaving', 'Hopefully the news will be good', 'I am definitely not going', 'He is indubitably a criminal'.

Adverbs of duration tell us how long something takes or lasts and include 'briefly', 'temporarily', 'long', 'indefinitely', 'always', 'permanently', 'forever', as in 'We stopped briefly for coffee', 'Have you known her long?', 'Her face is permanently disfigured', 'They have parted forever'.

Adverbs of emphasis add emphasis to the action described by the verb and include 'absolutely', 'certainly', 'positively', 'quite', 'really', 'simply', 'just', as in 'They absolutely detest each other', 'He positively adores her', 'She really wants to be forgiven', 'I simply must go now'

Interrogative adverbs ask questions and include 'where', 'when', 'how', and 'why', as in 'Where are you going?', 'When will you be back?', 'How will you get there?', 'Why have they asked you to go?' They are placed at the beginning of sentences, and such sentences always end with a question mark.

adverbial clauses are subordinate clauses that modify the main or principal clause by adding information about time, place, concession, condition, manner, purpose and result. They usually follow the main clause but most of them can be put in front of the main clause for reason of emphasis or style.

Adverbial clauses of time indicate the time of an event and are introduced by conjunctions such as 'after', 'as', 'as soon as', 'before', 'once', 'since', 'the minute', 'the moment', 'till', 'until', 'when', 'whenever, while', 'whilst', as in 'He left after the meal was over', 'She arrived as I was leaving', 'Once I recognized him I spoke to him', 'I recognized him the minute I saw him', 'We won't know until tomorrow' and 'The thief ran away when he saw the police'.

Adverbial clauses of place indicate the location of an event and are introduced by conjunctions such as 'where', 'wherever' or 'everywhere', as in 'He was miserable where he was', 'They left it where they found it', 'Wherever I went I saw signs of poverty' and 'Everywhere she goes she causes trouble'.

Adverbial clauses of concession contain a fact that contrasts in some way with the main clause and are introduced by conjunctions such as 'although', 'even though', 'though', 'whereas', 'while', 'whilst', as in 'I have to admire his speech, although I disagree with what he said', 'He does his best at school work even though he is not very good at it' and 'Whilst I myself do not like him I can understand why he is popular'.

Adverbial clauses of condition deal with possible situations and are introduced by the conjunctions 'if', 'only if', 'unless', 'as long as', 'providing', 'provided', as in 'If you had kept quiet they would not have known about the event', 'We cannot go unless we get permission', 'They can leave only if they have finished their work' and 'Provided he is feeling better he can leave hospital'. Inversion can be used in such clauses instead of a conjunction, as in 'Had you been present you would have been most amused' and 'Had he any sense he would leave now'.

Adverbial clauses of manner describe the way that someone behaves or the way in which something is done, and are introduced by conjunctions such as 'as', 'as if', 'as though', 'like', 'the way', as in 'Why does he behave as he does', 'He slurred his speech as though he were drunk' and 'He looked at her as if he hated her'.

Adverbial clauses of purpose indicate the intention someone has when doing something and is introduced by conjunctions such as 'to', 'in order to', 'so as to', 'so', 'so that', as in 'He did that just to upset her', 'They will have to work long hours in order to make that amount of money', 'They started to run so as to get home before it rained' and 'The firm reduced the number of staff in order that they might avoid bankruptcy'.

Adverbial clauses of reason explain why something happens or is done and are introduced by conjunctions such as 'because', 'since', 'as', as in 'We didn't go because the car broke down', 'As it was raining we had the party indoors' and 'since he has broken the school rules he should be punished'.

Adverbial clauses of result indicate the result of an event or situation and are introduced by the conjunctions 'so' or 'so that', as in 'He fell awkwardly so that he broke his leg' and 'She stumbled over her words so that the audience had difficulty understanding her'. *See* COMPARISON OF ADVERBS and COMPOUNDS.

aero- is a prefix meaning 'air', as in 'aerobics', 'aerodynamics', 'aeroplane' and 'aerospace', or 'aircraft', as in as in 'aerodrome', 'aeronaut'.

affix refers to an element that is added to a base or root word to form another word. **Affixes** can be in the form of 'prefixes' or 'suffixes'. 'Prefix' is an **affix** that is added to the beginning of a word. Thus *audio* in 'audiovisual' is both a prefix and an affix. 'Suffix' is an **affix** that is added to the end of a word. Thus *-aholic* in 'workaholic' is a 'suffix' and an **affix.**

agent noun refers to someone that is the 'doer' of the action of a verb. It is usually spelt ending in either *-er*, as 'enquirer', or in *-or*, as in 'investigator' and 'supervisor', but frequently either of these endings is acceptable, as 'adviser/advisor'.

agreement or **concord** refers to the agreeing of two or more elements in a clause or sentence, i.e. they take the same number, person or gender. In English the most common form of **agreement** is that between subject and verb, and this usually involves **number agreement**. This means that singular nouns are usually accompanied by singular verbs, as in 'She looks well', 'He is working late' and 'The boy has passed the exam', and that plural nouns are usually accompanied by plural verbs, as in 'They look well', 'They are working late' and 'The boys have passed the exam'.

Problems arise when the noun in question can be either singular or plural, for example, 'audience', 'committee', 'crowd', 'family', 'government', 'group'. Such nouns take a singular verb if the user is regarding the people or items referred to by the noun as a group, as in 'The family is moving house', or as individuals, as in 'The family are quarrelling over where to go on holiday'.

Compound subjects, that is two or more nouns acting as the subject, whether singular or plural, joined with 'and', are used with a plural noun, as in 'My friend and I are going to the cinema tonight' and 'James and John are leaving today', unless the two nouns together represent a single concept, as 'brandy and soda', in which case the verb is in the singular, as in 'Brandy and soda is his favourite drink' and 'cheese and pickle' in 'Cheese and pickle is the only sandwich filing available.

In cases where two or more singular nouns acting as the subject are connected with such phrases as 'as well as', 'together with' and 'plus', as in 'His mother, as well as his father, is away from home' and 'The flat, together with the house, is up for sale', the verb is in the singular.

Indefinite pronouns such as 'anyone', 'everyone', 'no one', 'someone', 'either', 'neither' are singular and should be followed by a singular verb, as in 'Each of the flats is self-contained', 'Everyone is welcome', 'No one is allowed in without a ticket' and 'Neither is quite what I am looking for'.

When the subject is a singular noun, which is separated from the verb by a number of plural nouns, as in 'a list of dates and times of the next concerts', the verb is in the singular because 'list' is singular, as in 'A list of dates and times of the next concerts is available'.

Agreement with reference to both number and gender affects pronouns, as in 'She blames herself', 'He could have kicked himself' and 'They asked themselves why they had got involved'. Problems arise when the pronoun is indefinite and so the sex of the person is unspecified. Formerly in such cases the masculine pronouns were assumed to be neutral and so 'Each of the pupils was asked to hand in his work' was considered quite acceptable. The rise of feminism has led to a questioning of this assumption and alternatives have been put forward. These include 'Each of the pupils was asked to hand in his/her (or his or her) work', but some people feel that this is clumsy. Another alternative is 'Each of the pupils was asked to hand in their work'. Although it is ungrammatical, this convention is becoming quite acceptable in modern usage. To avoid both the clumsiness of the former and the ungrammaticalness of the latter, it is possible to cast the whole sentence in the plural, as in 'All the pupils were asked to hand in their work'.

agro-, agri- is a prefix derived from Greek meaning 'field', as in 'agriculture', 'agribusiness', 'agrobiology', 'agrochemicals'.

-aholic is a suffix meaning 'addicted to', formed on analogy with 'alcoholic', as in 'workaholic', 'shopaholic'. It sometimes becomes -*oholic*, as in chocoholic.

allegory is a kind of story which has deeper significance as well as the obvious surface meaning of the story. It is usually used to get a moral message across symbolically. Two of the famous allegories in English literature are *Pilgrim's Progress* by John Bunyan (1628-88) and *The Faerie Queene* by Edmund Spenser (1552-99).

alliteration is a figure of speech in which a sequence of words begin with the same letter or sound as in 'Round and round the rugged rocks the ragged rascal ran' and 'Peter Piper picked a peck of pickled peppers'. The given examples are both tongue twisters but **alliteration** is frequently used by poets for literary effect as in a 'red, red rose'.

also is an adverb and should not be used as a conjunction instead of 'and'. Thus sentences such as 'Please send me some apples, also some pears' are grammatically incorrect.

although is a conjunction used to introduce a 'subordinate adverbial clause of concession', as in 'They are very happy although they are poor', meaning 'Despite the fact they are poor they are happy'. 'Though' or 'even though' can be substituted for 'although', as in 'they are very happy even though they are poor'. *See* ADVERBIAL CLAUSE and CONJUNCTION.

ambi- is a prefix derived from Greek 'two', 'both', as in 'ambidextrous', 'ambivalent'.

an *see* **indefinite article**.

an- *see* **a-**.

-ana is a suffix meaning 'things associated with', as in 'Victoriana', 'Americana'.

anacoluthon is a figure of speech which refers to a change of construction in a sentence before the original structure is complete, as in 'My feeling is—but you must decide for yourself—how long did you say you have?' **Anacoluthon** is usually found in spoken English when someone is thinking aloud. Unlike many figures of speech, it is usually used accidentally rather than for literary or rhetorical effect.

anadiplosis is a figure of speech which refers to the repetition of a word or group at the end of one phrase or sentence and the beginning of the next for literary effect, as in 'sit and think about the past—the past which had been so warm and happy'.

analogy is a figure of speech rather like the simile in which there is an inference of a resemblance between two items that are being compared, as in 'Mary's parties are a bit like Christmas—much looked forward to but often a bit of a disappointment'.

anastrophe is a figure of speech which refers to an inversion of the usual order of words in a sentence or phrase for emphasis, or literary or rhetorical effect, as in 'Many a foreign dawn has he seen'.

and is called a coordinating conjunction because it joins elements of language which are of equal status. The elements may be words, as in 'cows and horses', 'John and

James', 'provide wine and beer'; phrases, as in 'working hard and playing hard' and 'trying to look after her children and her elderly parents'; clauses, as in 'John has decided to emigrate and his brother has decided to join him' and 'He has lost his job and he now has no money'. When a coordinating conjunction is used, the subject of the second clause can sometimes be omitted if it is the same as the subject of the first clause, as in 'They have been forced to sell the house and are very sad about it'. *See* CONJUNCTION.

The use of **and** at the beginning of a sentence is disliked by many people. It should be used only for deliberate effect, as in 'And then he saw the monster', or in informal contexts.

Other coordinating conjunctions include 'but', 'or', 'yet', 'both... and', 'either... or', and 'neither.... nor', as in 'poor but honest' and 'the blue dress or the green one'.

Anglo- is a prefix meaning 'English', as in 'Anglo-Irish', 'Anglo-Indian'.

ante- is a prefix derived from Latin meaning 'before', as in 'antedate', 'antenatal', 'anteroom'.

antecedent refers to the noun or noun phrase in a main clause to which a relative pronoun in a relative clause refers back. Thus in the sentence 'People who live dangerously frequently get hurt', 'people' is an antecedent. Similarly, in the sentence 'The child identified the old man who attacked her', 'the old man' is the antecedent'. *See* RELATIVE CLAUSE.

anthropo- is a prefix derived from Greek meaning 'human being', as in anthropoid, anthropology.

anti- is a prefix derived from Greek meaning 'against'. It is used in many words that have been established in the language for a long time, as in 'antidote' and 'antipathy', but it has also been used to form modern words, as 'anti-establishment', 'antifreeze', 'anti-inflationary', 'anti-nuclear', 'anti-warfare'.

anticlimax is a figure of speech in which there is a sudden descent from the lofty to the ridiculous or the trivial, as in 'She went home in a flood of tears and a taxi' and Alexander Pope's 'When husbands or when lapdogs breathe their last'.

antiphrasis is a figure of speech in which a word or phrase is used in a sense that is opposite to the accepted sense. It is often used to achieve an ironic or humorous effect, as in 'His mother is ninety years young today'. Young is usually associated with youth but here it is associated with old age.

antithesis is a figure of speech in contrasting ideas are balanced for effect, as in 'We need money, not advice', 'More haste, less speed' and 'Marry at haste, repent at leisure'. It is a common figure of speech in literature, as in Alexander Pope's 'To err is human, to forgive, divine' and John Milton's 'Better to reign in hell than to serve in heaven'.

antonomasia is a figure of speech indicating the use of a personal name or proper name to anyone belonging to a class or group, as in 'John is such an Einstein that the other members of the class are in awe of him', where the meaning is that 'John has such a brilliant mind that the other members of the class are in awe of him'.

antonym refers to a word that is the opposite of another
word. Thus 'black' is an antonym for 'white', 'cowardly'
is an antonym for 'courageous' , 'dull' is an antonym for
'bright', and 'fast' is an antonym for 'slow'.

any is a pronoun which may take either a singular or plural
verb, depending on the context. When a singular noun is
used, a singular verb is used, as in 'Is any of the cloth still
usable?' 'Are any of the children coming?' When a plural
noun is used, either a plural or a singular verb can be used,
the singular verb being more formal, as in 'Did you ask if
any of his friends were/was there?'.

anyone should be used with a singular verb, as in 'Has anyone seen my book' and 'Is anyone coming to the lecture'.
It should also be followed, where relevant, by a singular,
not plural, personal pronoun or possessive adjective, as in
'Has anyone left his/her book'. Because this construction,
which avoids the sexist 'his', is considered by many people to be clumsy, there is a growing tendency to use
'their' and be ungrammatical.

aposiopesis is a figure of speech in which words are omitted or there is a sudden breaking off for dramatic effect, as
in 'The door slowly opened and....' and 'There was the
noise of gunshot and then....'

apostrophe¹ is a figure of speech which takes the form of a
rhetorical address to an absent or dead person or to a per-
sonified thing, as in 'O Romeo! Romeo! wherefore art
thou, Romeo?' and 'Oh Peace, why have you deserted
us?'

apostrophe² is a form of punctuation that is mainly used to
indicate possession. Many spelling errors centre on the

position of the apostrophe in relation to *s*.

Possessive nouns are usually formed by adding *'s* to the singular noun, as in 'the girl's mother', and Peter's car'; by adding an apostrophe to plural nouns that end in *s*, as in 'all the teachers' cars'; by adding *'s* to irregular plural nouns that do not end in *s*, as in 'women's shoes'.

In the possessive form of a name or singular noun that ends in *s*, *x* or *z*, the apostrophe may or may not be followed by *s*. In words of one syllable the final *s* is usually added, as in 'James's house', 'the fox's lair', 'Roz's dress'. The final *s* is most frequently omitted in names, particularly in names of three or more syllables, as in 'Euripides' plays'. In many cases the presence or absence of final *s* is a matter of convention.

The apostrophe is also used to indicate omitted letters in contracted forms of words, as in 'can't' and 'you've'. They are sometimes used to indicate missing century numbers in dates, as in 'the '60s and '70s', but are not used at the end of decades, etc, as in '1960s', not '1960's'.

Generally apostrophes are no longer used to indicate omitted letters in shortened forms that are in common use, as in 'phone' and 'flu'.

Apostrophes are often omitted wrongly in modern usage, particularly in the media and by advertisers, as in 'womens hairdressers', 'childrens helpings'. In addition, apostrophes are frequently added erroneously (as in 'potato's for sale' and 'Beware of the dog's'). This is partly because people are unsure about when and when not to use them and partly because of a modern tendency to punctuate as little as possible.

apposition refers to a noun or a phrase which provides further information about another noun or phrase. Both nouns and phrases refer to the same person or thing. In the phrase 'Peter Jones, our managing director', ' Peter Jones' and 'our managing director' are said to be in **apposition**. Similarly, in the phrase 'his cousin, the chairman of the firm', 'his cousin' and 'the chairman of the firm' are in **apposition.**

arch- is a prefix derived from Greek meaning 'chief', as in 'archbishop', 'archduke', 'arch-enemy'.

-arch is a suffix derived from the Greek meaning 'chief, ruler', as in 'anarchy', 'hierarchy' and 'monarchy'.

-arian is a suffix derived from Latin and means, in one of its senses, 'a supporter of', as in 'vegetarian', or 'one connected with', as in 'antiquarian' and 'librarian'.

article *see* **definite article** and **indefinite article**.

as is a conjunction which can introduce either a 'subordinate adverbial clause of time', as in 'I caught sight of him as I was leaving', a 'subordinate adverbial clause of manner', as in 'He acted as he promised', and 'a subordinate adverbial clause of reason', as in 'As it's Saturday he doesn't have to work'. it is also used in the **as....as** construction, as in 'She doesn't play as well as her sister does'.

    The construction may be followed by a subject pronoun or an object pronoun, according to sense. In the sentence 'He plays as well as she', which is a slightly shortened form of 'She plays as well as he does', 'he' is a subject pronoun. In informal English the subject pronoun often becomes an object pronoun, as in 'She plays as well as him'. In the sentence 'They hate their father as much as her', 'her' is an object and the sentence means 'They hate their father as much as they hate her', but in the sentence 'They hate their father as much as she', 'she' is a subject and the sentence means 'They hate their father as much as she does'. *See* ADVERBIAL CLAUSE and CONJUNCTION.

assonance is a figure of speech in which vowel sounds are repeated to give a half-rhyme effect, as in 'with gun, drum, trumpet, blunderbuss and thunder'.

astro- is a prefix derived from Greek meaning 'star', as in 'astrology', 'astronomy', 'astronaut', 'astrophysics'.

asyndeton is a figure of speech referring to the omission of conjunctions for dramatic or literary effect, as in 'I came, I saw, I conquered' and 'He entered, he looked round, he left'.

-athon, -thon is a suffix meaning 'large scale or long-lasting contest or event', as in 'swimathon', 'telethon'. These words are formed on analogy with the Greek derived word 'marathon', and they often refer to events undertaken for charity.

attributive adjective refers to an **adjective** that is placed immediately before the noun which it qualifies. In the phrases 'a red dress', 'the big house' and 'an enjoyable evening', 'red, 'big' and 'enjoyable' are attributive adjectives.

audio- is derived from Latin 'hear'. It is found in several words that have been established in the language for a long time, as in 'auditory', 'audition', but it is also used to form many modern words, as in 'audiotape', 'audio-cassette' and 'audiovisual'.

auto- is a prefix derived from Greek meaning 'of or by itself', as in 'autobiography' and 'autograph'. It is also
used to refer to things that work by themselves 'automatically', as in 'automobile', 'autocue', 'automaton', and to
things that have to do with cars, as in 'automobiles',
'autosport', 'autotheft'.

auxiliary verb refers to a verb which is used in forming
tenses, moods and voices of other verbs. These include
'be', 'do' and 'have'.

The verb 'to be' is used as an **auxiliary verb** with the -
ing form of the main verb to form the continuous present
tense, as in 'They are living abroad just now' and 'We
were thinking of going on holiday but we changed our
minds'.

The verb 'to be' is used as an **auxiliary verb** with the
past participle of the main verb to form the passive voice,
as in 'Her hands were covered in blood' and 'These toys
are manufactured in China'.

The verb 'to have' is used as an **auxiliary verb** along
with the past participle of the main verb to form the perfect tenses, as in 'They have filled the post', 'She had realized her mistake' and 'They wished that they had gone
earlier'.

The verb 'to be' is used as an **auxiliary verb** along with
the main verb to form negative sentences, as in 'She is not
accepting the job'. The verb 'to do' is used as an **auxiliary verb** along with the main verb to form negative sentences, as in 'he does not believe her'. It is also used along
with the main verb to form questions, as in 'Does he know
that she's gone?' and to form sentences in which the verb

is emphasized, as in 'She *does* want to go'. *See* **modal auxiliary**.

B

back formation refers to the process of forming a new word by removing an element from an existing word. This is the reversal of the usual process since many words are formed by adding an element to a base or root word. Examples of **back formation** include 'burgle' from 'burglary'; 'caretake' from 'caretaker'; 'donate' from 'donation; 'eavesdrop' from 'eavesdropper'; 'enthuse' from 'enthusiasm'; 'intuit' from 'intuition'; 'liaise' from 'liaison'; 'reminisce' from 'reminiscence'; 'televise' from 'television'.

base refers to the basic uninflected form of a verb. It is found as the infinitive form, as in 'to go' and 'to take', and as the imperative form, as in 'Go away!' and 'Take it!' It is also the form that the verb in the present indicative tense takes, except for the third person singular, as in 'I always go there on a Sunday' and 'They go there regularly.' **Base** also refers to the basic element in word formation. In this sense it is also known as 'root' or 'stem'. For example, in 'infectious' 'infect' is the base, in 'indescribable' 'describe' is the base and in 'enthusiastic' 'enthuse' is the base.

bathos is a figure of speech consisting of sudden descent from the lofty or noble to the ridiculous or trivial. This descent can be either intentional for comic or satiric effect, as in Alexander Pope's 'When husbands or when lapdogs breathe their last', or it can be accidental, as in 'She collected her children and her coat'. **Bathos** and 'anticlimax' mean the same. *See* **anticlimax**.

be *see* **auxiliary verb**.

both can be used as determiner, as in 'He broke both his arms' and 'He lost both his sons in the war'; a pronoun, as in 'I don't mind which house we rent. I like them both' and 'Neither of them work here. The boss sacked them both'; a conjunction, as in 'He both likes and admires her' and 'She is both talented and honest'. **Both** can sometimes be followed by 'of'. 'Both their children are grown up' and 'Both of their children are grown up' are both acceptable. Care should be taken to avoid using **both** unnecessarily. In the sentence 'The two items are both identical', **both** is redundant.

because is a conjunction that introduces a subordinate adverbial clause of reason', as in 'They sold the house because they are going abroad' and 'Because she is shy she never goes to parties'. It is often used incorrectly in such constructions as 'The reason they went away is because they were bored'. This should be rephrased as either 'The reason that they went away is that they were bored' or 'They went away because they were bored'.

before can either be a preposition, an adverb or a conjunction. As a preposition it means either 'coming or going in front of in time', as in 'He was the chairman before this one', or coming or going in front of in place, as in 'She went before him into the restaurant'. As an adverb it means 'at a time previously', as in 'I told you before' and 'He has been married before'. As a conjunction it introduces a 'subordinate adverbial clause of time', as in 'The guests arrived before she was ready for them' and 'Before I knew it they had arrived'.

bi- is a prefix derived from Latin meaning 'two', as in 'bicycle', 'bifocal', 'bilingual', 'binoculars', 'bisect'. **Bi-** forms words in English in which it means 'half', and other words in which it means 'twice'. This can give rise to confusion in such words as 'biweekly' and 'bimonthly', where there are two possible sets of meanings. 'Biweekly' can mean either 'every two weeks' or 'twice a week' so that one would not be able to be certain about the frequency of a 'biweekly' publication. Similarly, a 'bimonthly' publication might appear either twice a month or once every two months.

biblio- is a prefix derived from Greek meaning 'book', as in 'bibliophile' (a person who is fond of or collects books) and 'bibliography'.

bio- is a prefix derived from Greek meaning life or living material, as in 'biography', 'biology', 'biochemistry', 'biodegradable', 'biosphere', 'biopsy'.

blend refers to a word formed by the merging of two other words or elements, as in 'brunch' from 'breakfast' and 'lunch'; 'camcorder' from 'camera' and 'recorder'; 'chocoholic' from 'chocolate' and 'alcoholic'; 'motel' from 'motor' and 'hotel'; 'smog' from 'smoke' and 'fog'; 'televangelist' from 'television' and 'evangelist'.

bold or **bold face** refers to a typeface that is thick and black. It is used for emphasis or to highlight certain words. The headwords or entry words in this book are set in bold type.

book titles cause problems as to punctuation. How they are treated in publications, business reports, etc, depends largely on the house style of the firm concerned. However, they are generally written in documents, letters, etc, as they appear on their title pages, that is with the first letter of the first word and of the following main words of the title in capital letters, and those of words of lesser importance, such as the articles, prepositions and coordinate conjunctions, in lowercase letters, as in The Guide to Yoga, Hope for the Best and In the Middle of Life.

Some people, and some house-style manuals, prefer to put the titles in italic, as in *A Room with a View* and *A Guide to Dental Health*. Others prefer to put book titles in quotation marks, as in 'Gardening for Beginners'. Such a convention can make use of either single or double quotation marks. Thus either 'Desserts for the Summer' or "Desserts for the Summer" is possible provided that the writer is consistent throughout any one piece of writing. If the title of a book is mentioned in a piece of direct speech in quotation marks it goes within the opposite style of quotation marks from the piece in direct speech. Thus if the direct speech is within single quotation marks, the book title goes within double quotation marks, as in 'Have you read "Wuthering Heights" or are you not a Bronte fan?' If the direct speech is within double quotation marks, the book title goes between single quotation marks, as in "Would you say that 'Animal Farm' was your favourite Orwell novel?"

It is even quite common for book titles to appear in documents both in italic type and with quotation marks. To some extent the punctuation of book titles is a matter of choice as long as they are consistent, but there is a growing tendency to have as little punctuation as possible and to have as uncluttered a page as possible.

borrowing refers to the taking over of a word from a foreign language and also refers to the word so borrowed. Many words borrowed into English are totally assimilated as to spelling and pronunciation. Others remain obviously different and retain their own identity as to spelling or pronunciation, as 'raison d'être', borrowed from French. Many of them have been so long part of the English language, such as since the Norman Conquest, that they are no longer thought of as being foreign words. However the process goes on, and recent borrowings include 'glasnost' and 'perestroika' from Russian.

French, Latin and Greek have been the main sources of our **borrowings** over the centuries. However, we have borrowed extensively from other languages as well. These include Italian, from which we have borrowed many terms relating to music, art and architecture. These include 'piano', 'libretto', 'opera', 'soprano', 'tempo', 'corridor', 'fresco', 'niche', 'parapet' and 'grotto', as well as many food terms such as 'macaroni', 'pasta', 'semolina' and 'spaghetti'.

From the Dutch we have acquired many words relating to the sea and ships since they were a great sea-faring nation. These include 'cruise', 'deck', 'skipper' and 'yacht'. Through the Dutch/Afrikaans connection we have borrowed 'apartheid', 'boss' and 'trek'.

From German we have borrowed 'dachshund', 'hamster', 'frankfurter', 'kindergarten' and 'waltz', as well as some words relating to World War II, for example, 'blitz', 'flak' and 'strafe'.

From Norse and the Scandinavian languages have come a wide variety of common words, such as 'egg', 'dirt', 'glitter', 'kick', 'law', 'odd', 'skill', 'take', 'they', 'though', as well as some more modern sporting terms such as 'ski' and 'slalom'.

From the Celtic languages have come 'bannock', 'bog', 'brogue', 'cairn', 'clan', 'crag', 'slogan' and 'whisky', and from Arabic have come 'algebra', 'alkali', 'almanac', 'apricot', 'assassin', 'cypher', 'ghoul', 'hazard', 'mohair', 'safari', 'scarlet' and 'talisman'.

The Indian languages have provided us with many words, originally from the significant British presence there in the days of the British Empire. They include 'bungalow', 'chutney', 'dinghy', 'dungarees', 'gymkhana', 'jungle', 'pundit' and 'shampoo'. In modern times there has been an increasing interest in Indian food and cookery, and words such as 'pakora', 'poppadom', 'samosa', etc, have come into the language.

From the South American languages have come 'avocado', 'chocolate', 'chilli', 'potato', 'tobacco' and 'tomato'. From Hebrew have come 'alphabet', 'camel', 'cinnamon' and 'maudlin', as well as more modern borrowings from Yiddish such as 'bagel', 'chutzpah', 'schmaltz' and 'schmuck'.

From the native North American languages have come

'anorak', 'kayak', 'raccoon' and 'toboggan', and from the Aboriginal language of Australia have come 'boomerang' and 'kangaroo'.

'Judo', 'bonsai', and 'tycoon' have come from Japanese, 'rattan' from Malay and 'kung-fu', 'sampan' and 'ginseng' from Chinese.

The borrowing process continues. With Britain becoming more of a cosmopolitan and multi-cultural nation the borrowing is increasing.

-bound is a suffix meaning 'confined or restricted', as in housebound, snowbound and spellbound. It can also mean 'obligated', as in 'duty-bound'.

brackets are used to enclose information that is in some way additional to the main statement. The information so enclosed is called 'parenthesis' and the pair of brackets enclosing it can be known as 'parentheses'. The information that is enclosed in the brackets is purely supplementary or explanatory in nature and could be removed without changing the overall basic meaning or grammatical completeness of the statement. **Brackets**, like 'commas' and 'dashes', interrupt the flow of the main statement but **brackets** indicate a more definite or clear-cut interruption. The fact that they are more visually obvious emphasizes this.

Material within brackets can be one word, as in 'In a local wine bar we had some delicious crepes (pancakes)' and 'They didn't have the chutzpah (nerve) to challenge her'. It can also take the form of dates, as in 'Robert Louis Stevenson (1850-94) wrote *Treasure Island*' and '*Animal Farm* was written by George Orwell (1903-50)'.

brackets 42

The material within brackets can also take the form of a phrase, as in 'They served lasagne (a kind of pasta) and some delicious veal' and 'They were drinking Calvados (a kind of brandy made from apples)' or in the form of a clause, as in 'We were to have supper (or so they called it) later in the evening' and 'They went for a walk round the loch (as a lake is called in Scotland) before taking their departure'.

It can also take the form of a complete sentence, as in 'He was determined (we don't know why) to tackle the problem alone' and 'She made it clear (nothing could be more clear) that she was not interested in the offer'. Sentences that appear in brackets in the middle of a sentence are not usually given an initial capital letter or a full stop, as in 'They very much desired (she had no idea why) to purchase her house'. If the material within brackets comes at the end of a sentence the full stop comes outside the second bracket, as in 'For some reason we agreed to visit her at home (we had no idea where she lived)'.

If the material in the brackets is a sentence which comes between two other sentences it is treated like a normal sentence with an initial capital letter and a closing full stop, as in 'He never seems to do any studying. (He is always either asleep or watching television.) Yet he does brilliantly in his exams.' Punctuation of the main statement is unaffected by the presence of the brackets and their enclosed material except that any punctuation that would have followed the word before the first bracket follows the second bracket, as in 'He lives in a place (I am not sure exactly where), that is miles from anywhere.

There are various shapes of brackets. Round brackets are the most common type. Square brackets are sometimes used to enclose information that is contained inside other information already in brackets, as in '(Christopher Marlowe [1564-93] was a contemporary of Shakespeare)' or in a piece of writing where round brackets have already been used for some other purpose. Thus in a dictionary if round brackets are used to separate off the pronunciation, square brackets are sometimes used to separate off the etymologies.

Square brackets are also used for editorial comments in a scholarly work where the material within brackets is more of an intrusion to the flow of the main statement than is normerly the case with bracketed material. Angle brackets and brace brackets tend to be used in more scholarly or technical contexts.

buildings can cause problems with regard to the style and punctuation of their names. The proper name attached to the building should have an initial capital, as should the common noun that may be part of it, as in The White House, The Saltire Building, The National Portrait Gallery and The Museum of Childhood.

businesses and **organizations** often cause style and punctuation problems with regard to their names or titles. In general the initial letters of the main words of the title should be in capital letters and the words of lesser importance, such as the articles, coordinating conjunctions and prepositions, should be in lower case, except when they are the first word of the title, as in 'The Indian Carpet Company', 'Kitchens for All' and 'Capital Industrial

Cleaners'. Obviously, when the names of people are involved these should have initial capital letters, as in 'Jones and Brown'.

but is a conjunction that connects two opposing ideas. It is a 'coordinating conjunction' in that it connects two elements of equal status. The elements may be words, as in 'not James but John'; phrases, as in 'working hard but not getting anywhere' and 'trying to earn a living but not succeeding'; clauses, as in 'He has arrived but his sister is late', 'I know her but I have never met him' and 'He likes reading but she prefers to watch TV'. It should not be used when no element of contrast is present. Thus the following sentence should be rephrased, at least in formal English—'She is not professionally trained but taught herself'. The two clauses are in fact agreeing, not disagreeing, with each other and so, strictly speaking, **but** should not be used.

The use of **but** at the beginning of a sentence is disliked by many people. It should be used only for deliberate effect or in informal contexts.

by- is a prefix meaning 'subordinate', 'secondary', 'incidental', as in by-product, by-road, by-effect. It can also mean 'around', as in by-pass.

C

capital letters are much less common than lower-case letters. They are used as the initial letter of proper nouns. Thus names of countries, rivers, mountains, cities, etc. Thus we find Africa, Mount Everest, River Nile, Paris, etc. The first names and surnames of people have initial capital letters, as in John Black and Mary Brown. Initial capital letters are used for the days of the week, as in Tuesday and Wednesday, for the months of the year, as in May and October, public and religious holidays, as in Easter Sunday, Ramadan and Hanaku. Initial capital letters are used for the books of the Bible.

Points of the compass are spelt with an initial capital letter if they are part of a specific geographical feature or region, as in South Africa.

Initial capital letters are usually used in the titles of books. Only the main words are capitalized. Prepositions, determiners and the articles are left in lower-case, unless they form the first word of the title, as in *A Room with a View* and *For Whom the Bell Tolls*—*see* BOOK TITLES.

Initial capital letters are necessary in tradenames, as in Hoover, Jacuzzi, Xerox and Kodak. Note that verbs formed from trade names are not spelt with an initial capital letter.

The first word in a sentence is spelt with a capital letter, as in 'We heard them come in. They made very little noise. However, we are light sleepers.'.

For capital letters in direct speech see DIRECT SPEECH. For capital letters in abbreviation and acronyms see ABBREVIATIONS and ACRONYMS.

cardi- is a prefix derived from Greek meaning 'heart', as in 'cardiology', 'cardiac'.

cardinal number refers to numbers such as one, two three, etc, as opposed to 'ordinal numbers' which refer to numbers such as first, second, third, etc.

clause refers to a group of words containing a finite verb which forms part of a compound or complex sentence. See MAIN CLAUSE, SUBORDINATE CLAUSES, ADVERBIAL CLAUSES, NOUN CLAUSES and RELATIVE **clauses**.

clerihew is a humorous four-line light verse in which the first two lines rhyme with each other and the last two rhyme with each other. The clerihew was popularized by Edward Clerihew Bentley (1875-1956). It usually deals with a person named in the first line and then describes him in a humorous way, as in

Mr Michael Foot
Had lots of loot
He loved to gloat
While petting his stoat

cliché is a hackneyed stereotyped expression which is much overused. Examples of clichés include 'unaccustomed as I am to public speaking', 'the light at the end of the tunnel' and 'All's well that ends well'.

collective noun refers to a group of things or people. It is used when the whole group is being considered, as in 'flock of sheep', 'herd of cattle', 'team of oxen', 'shoal of herring', 'covey of partridges', 'unkindness of ravens', 'gaggle of geese', 'pride of lions', 'mutation of thrushes', 'exaltation of larks', 'convocation of eagles'.

colloquial refers to informal language, such as that found in informal conversation.

colon is a punctuation mark (:) which is used within a sentence to explain, interpret, clarify or amplify what has gone before it. 'The standard of school work here is extremely high: it is almost university standard', 'The fuel bills are giving cause for concern: they are almost double last year's'. 'We have some new information: the allies have landed'. A capital letter is not usually used after the colon in this context.

The **colon** is also used to introduce lists or long quotations, as in 'The recipe says we need: tomatoes, peppers, courgettes, garlic, oregano and basil', 'The boy has a huge list of things he needs for school: blazer, trousers, shirts, sweater, ties, shoes, tennis shoes, rugby boots, sports clothes and leisure wear' and 'One of his favourite quotations was: "If music be the food of love play on"'.

The **colon** is sometimes used in numerals, as in '7:30 a.m.', '22:11:72' and 'a ratio of 7:3'. It is used in the titles of some books, for example where there is a subtitle or explanatory title, as in 'The Dark Years: the Economy in the 1930s.

In informal writing, the dash is sometimes used instead of the colon, Indeed the dash tends to be overused for this purpose.

comma is a very common punctuation mark. In modern usage there is a tendency to adopt a system of minimal
punctuation and the comma is one of the casualties of this
new attitude. Most people use the comma considerably
less frequently than was formerly the case.

However there are certain situations in which the
comma is still commonly used. One of these concerns
lists. The individual items in a series of three or more
items are separated by commas. Whether a comma is put
before the 'and' which follows the second-last item is
now a matter of choice. Some people dislike the use of a
comma after 'and' in this situation, and it was formerly
considered wrong. Examples of lists include—'at the
sports club we can play tennis, squash, badminton and table tennis', 'We need to buy bread, milk, fruit and sugar',
and 'They are studying French, German, Spanish and
Russian'. The individual items in a list can be quite long,
as in 'We opened the door, let ourselves in, fed the cat and
started to cook a meal' and 'They consulted the map,
planned the trip, got some foreign currency and were
gone before we realized it'. Confusion may arise if the
last item in the list contains 'and' in its own right, as in 'In
the pub they served ham salad, shepherd's pie, pie and
chips and omelette. In such cases it as well to put a
comma before the 'and'.

In cases where there is a list of adjectives before a noun,
the use of commas is now optional although it was formerly standard practice. Thus both 'She wore a long, red,
sequinned dress' and 'She wore a long red sequinned
dress' are used. When the adjective immediately before

the noun has a closer relationship with it than the other adjectives no comma should be used, as in 'a beautiful old Spanish village'.

The **comma** is used to separate clauses or phrases that are parenthetical or naturally cut off from the rest of a sentence, as in 'My mother, who was of Irish extraction, was very superstitious'. In such a sentence the clause within the commas can be removed without altering the basic meaning. Care should be taken to include both commas. Commas are not normally used to separate main clauses and relative clauses, as in 'The woman whom I met was my friend's sister'. Nor are they usually used to separate main clauses and subordinate clauses, as in 'He left when we arrived' and 'They came to the party although we didn't expect them to'. If the subordinate clause precedes the main clause, it is sometimes followed by a comma, especially if it is a reasonably long clause, as in 'Although we stopped and thought about it, we still made the wrong decision'. If the clause is quite short, or if it is a short phrase, a comma is not usually inserted, as in 'Although it rained we had a good holiday' and 'Although poor they were happy'. The use of commas to separate such words and expression from the rest of the sentence to which they are related is optional. Thus one can write 'However, he could be right' or 'However he could be right'. The longer the expression is, the more likely it is to have a comma after it, as in 'On the other hand, we may decide not to go'.

Commas are always used to separate terms of address, interjections or question tags from the rest of the sentence, as in 'Please come this way, Ms Brown, and make yourself at home', 'Now, ladies, what can I get you?' and 'It's cold today, isn't it?'

Commas may be used to separate main clauses joined by a coordinating conjunction, but this is not usual if the clauses have the same subject or object, as in 'She swept the floor and dusted the table'. In cases where the subjects are different and the clauses are fairly long, it is best to insert a comma, as in 'They took all the furniture with them and she was left with nothing'.

A **comma** can be inserted to avoid repeating a verb in the second of two clause, as in 'he plays golf and tennis his brother rugby'.

commands are expressed in the imperative mood, as in 'Be quiet!', 'Stop crying!', 'Go away!'

common nouns are simply the names of ordinary, everyday non-specific things and people, as opposed to proper nouns which refer to the names of particular individuals or specific places. **Common nouns** include 'baby', 'cat', 'girl', 'hat', 'park', 'sofa' and 'table'.

comparison of adjectives is achieved in two different ways. Some adjectives form their comparative by adding -*er* to the positive or absolute form, as in 'braver', 'louder', 'madder', 'shorter' and 'taller'. Other adjectives form their comparative by using 'more' in conjunction with them, as in 'more beautiful', 'more realistic', 'more suitable', and 'more tactful'. Which is the correct form is largely a matter of length. One-syllable adjectives, such as 'loud', add -*er*, as 'louder'. Two-syllable adjectives sometimes have both forms as a possibility, as in 'gentler/

more gentle', and 'cleverest/most clever'. Adjectives with three or more syllables usually form their comparatives with 'more', as in 'more comfortable', 'more gracious', 'more regular', and 'more understanding'. Some adjectives are irregular in their comparative forms, as in 'good/better', 'bad/worse', 'many/more'. Only if they begin with *un-* are they likely to end in *-er*, as in 'untrustworthier'.

Some adjectives by their very definitions do not normally have a comparative form, for example 'unique'.

complement is the equivalent of 'object' in a clause with a linking or copula verb. In the sentence 'Jack is a policeman', 'a policeman' is the **complement**. In the sentence 'Jane is a good mother', 'a good mother' is the complement', and in the sentence 'His son is an excellent football player', 'an excellent football player' is the complement.

complex sentence refers to a type of sentence in which there is a main clause and one or more subordinate clauses. The sentence 'We went to visit him although he had been unfriendly to us' is a complex sentence since it is composed of a main clause and one subordinate clause ('although he had been unfriendly to us'). The sentence 'We wondered where he had gone and why he was upset' is a complex sentence since it has a main clause and two subordinate clauses ('where he had gone' and 'why he was upset').

compound sentence refers to a type of sentence with more than one clause and linked by a coordinating conjunction, such as 'and' or 'but', as in 'He applied for a new job and got it' and 'I went to the cinema but I didn't enjoy the film'.

concord *see* **number agreement**.

concrete noun refers to something which one can touch, as opposed to an 'abstract noun' which one cannot. **Concrete nouns** include 'bag', 'glass', 'plate', 'pot', 'clothes', 'field', 'garden', 'flower', 'potato', 'foot' and 'shoe'. *See* ABSTRACT NOUN.

conjunctions are of two types. Coordinating conjunctions join units of equal status, as in 'bread and butter', 'We asked for some food and we got it'. A subordinating conjunction joins a dependent or subordinating clause to main verbs: in 'We asked him why he was there', 'why he was there' is a subordinate clause and thus 'why' is a subordinating conjunction.

continuous tenses *see* **tense**.

copula *see* **linking verb**.

copular verb *see* **linking verb**.

count noun is the same as COUNTABLE NOUN.

countable noun is one which can be preceded by 'a' and can take a plural, as in 'hat/hats', 'flower/flowers'. *See also* UNCOUNTABLE NOUN.

D

dangling participle is one that has been misplaced in a sentence. A participle is often used to introduce a phrase which is attached to a subject mentioned later in a sentence, as in 'Worn out by the long walk, she fell to the ground in a faint'. 'Worn out' is the participle and 'she' the subject. Another example is 'Laughing in glee at having won, she ordered some champagne'. In this sentence 'laughing' is the participle and 'she' is the subject. It is a common error for such a participle not to be related to any subject, as in 'Imprisoned in the dark basement, it seemed a long time since she had seen the sun'. This participle is said to be 'dangling'. Another example of a **dangling participle** is contained in 'Living alone, the days seemed long'.

It is also a common error for a participle to be related to the wrong subject in a sentence, as in 'Painting the ceiling, some of the plaster fell on his head', 'Painting' is the participle and should go with a subject 'he'. Instead it goes with 'some of the plaster'. Participles in this situation are more correctly known as 'misrelated participles', although they are also called **dangling participles.**

dash is a punctuation mark in the form of a short line that indicates a short break in the continuity of a sentence, as in 'He has never been any trouble at school—quite the reverse', 'I was amazed when he turned up—I thought he was still abroad'. In such situations it serves the same purpose as brackets, except that it is frequently considered more informal. The dash should be used sparingly. Depending on it too much can lead to careless writing with ideas set down at random rather than turned into a piece of coherent prose.

The **dash** can be used to emphasize a word or phrase, as in 'They said goodbye then—forever'. It can also be used to add a remark to the end of a sentence, as in 'They had absolutely no money—a regular state of affairs towards the end of the month.' The **dash** can also be used to introduce a statement that amplifies or explains what has been said, as in 'The burglars took everything of value—her jewellery, the silver, the TV set, her hi-fi and several hundred pounds.' It can be used to summarize what has gone before, as in 'Disease, poverty, ignorance—these are the problems facing us.'

The **dash** is also used to introduce an afterthought, as in 'You can come with me—but you might not want to'. It can also introduce a sharp change of subject, as in 'I'm just making tea—what was that noise?' It can also be used to introduce some kind of balance in a sentence, as in 'It's going to take two of us to get this table out of here—one to move it and one to hold the door open.'

The **dash** is sometimes found in pairs. A pair of dashes acts in much the same way as a set of round brackets. A pair of dashes can be used to indicate a break in a sentence, as in 'We prayed—prayed as we had never prayed

before—that the children would be safe', 'It was—on re-
flection—his best performance yet', and 'He introduced
me to his wife—an attractive pleasant woman—before he
left'.

Dashes are used to indicate hesitant speech, as in 'I
don't—well—maybe—you could be right'. They can be
used to indicate the omission of part of a word or name, as
in 'It's none of your b—business.', 'He's having an affair
with Mrs D–'.

They can also be used between points in time or space,
as in 'Edinburgh—London' and '1750—1790.'

dates are usually written in figures, as in 1956, rather than
in words, as in nineteen fifty-six, except in formal contexts, such as legal documents. There are various ways of
writing dates. The standard form in Britain is becoming
day followed by month followed by year, as in '24 February 1970'. In America the standard form of this is 'February 24 1970', and that is a possibility in Britain also. Alternatively, some people write '24th February 1970'. Care
should be taken with the writing of dates entirely in numbers, especially if one is corresponding with someone in
America. In Britain the day of the month is put first, the
month second and the year third, as in '2/3/50', '2 March
1950'. In America the month is put first, followed by the
day of the month and the year. Thus in America '2/3/50'
would be 3 February 1950.

Centuries may be written either in figures, as in 'the
19th century', or in words, as in 'the nineteenth century'.

Decades and centuries are now usually written without
apostrophes. as in '1980s' and '1990s'.

dative case refers to the case which indicates 'to' or 'for'. This is applicable to Latin but not to English, where such meanings are expressed by prepositional phrases. In English the 'indirect object' is equivalent to the **dative case** in some situations.

deca- is a prefix derived from Greek meaning 'ten', as in 'decade', 'decathlon' and 'decahedron'.

deci- is a prefix derived from Latin meaning 'tenth', as in 'decibel', 'decimal', 'decimate' and 'decilitre'.

declarative sentence refers to a sentence which conveys information. The subject precedes the verb in it. Examples include 'They won the battle', 'He has moved to another town', 'Lots of people go there' and 'There is a new person in charge'. **Declarative mood** is the same as **indicative mood**.

declension refers to the variation of the form of a noun, adjective or pronoun to show different cases, such as nominative and accusative. It also refers to the class into which such words are placed, as in first declension, second declension, etc. The term applies to languages such as Latin but is not applicable to English.

definite article is a term for 'the', which is the most frequently used word in the English language. 'The' is used to refer back to a person or thing that has already been mentioned, as in 'Jack and Jill built a model. The model was of a ship' and 'We've bought a car. It was the cheapest car we could find'.

'The' can be used to make a general statement about all things of a particular type, as in 'The computer has lead to the loss of many jobs' and 'The car has caused damage to the environment'. 'The' can be used to refer to a whole class or group, as in 'the Italians', 'the Browns' and 'the younger generation'.

'The' can also be used to refer to services or systems, as in 'They are not on the phone' and 'She prefers going by bus'. It can be used to refer to the name of a musical instrument when someone's ability to play it is being referred to, as in 'Her son is learning to play the violin'.

'The' indicates a person or thing to be the only one, as in the Bible, the King of Spain, the White House, the Palace of Westminster and the President of the United States.

'The' can be used instead of a possessive determiner to refer to parts of the body, as in 'She took him by the arm' and 'The dog bit him on the leg'.

'The' is used in front of superlative adjectives, as in 'the largest amount of money' and 'the most beautiful woman'. It can also be used to indicate that a person or thing is unique or exceptional, as in 'the political debater of his generation'. In this last sense 'the' is pronounced 'thee'.

degree refers to a level of comparison of gradable adjectives. The degrees of comparison comprise 'absolute' or 'positive', as in 'big', 'calm', 'dark', 'fair', 'hot', 'late', 'short' and 'tall'; 'comparative', as in 'bigger', 'calmer', 'darker', 'fairest', 'hotter', 'late', 'shorter' and 'taller'; 'superlative', as in 'biggest', 'calmest', 'darkest', 'fairest', 'hottest', 'latest', 'shortest' and 'tallest'.

Degree can also refer to adverbs. 'Adverbs of degree' include 'extremely', 'very', 'greatly', 'rather', 'really', 'remarkably', 'terribly', as in 'an extremely rare case', 'a very old man', 'He's remarkably brave' and 'We're terribly pleased'.

demi- is a prefix derived from old French meaning 'half', as in 'demigod' and 'demijohn'.

demonstrative determiners are used to indicate things or people in relationship to the speaker or writer in space or time. 'This' and 'these' indicate nearness to the speaker, as in 'Will you take this book home?' and 'These flowers are for you'. 'That' and 'those' indicate distance from the speaker, as in 'Get that creature out of here!' and 'Aren't those flowers over there beautiful!'

demonstrative pronouns are similar to **demonstrative determiners** except that they stand alone in place of a noun rather than preceding a noun, as in 'I'd like to give you this', 'What is that?', 'These are interesting books' and 'Those are not his shoes'.

dependent clause refers to a clause which cannot stand alone and make sense, unlike an independent or main clause. **Dependent clauses** depend on the main clause. The term is the same as 'subordinate clause'. *See* SUBORDINATE CLAUSE.

derivation has two meanings. It can refer to the etymology of a word, as in 'The derivation of the expression is unknown'. It can also refer to the process of forming a new word by adding an affix of some kind to an existing word or base, as in 'helpless' from 'help' and 'maker' from 'make'.

derivative refers to a word formed by **derivation**. For example, 'sweetly' is a derivative of 'sweet', 'peaceful' is a derivative from 'peace', 'clinging' from 'cling' and 'shortest' from 'short'.

derm- is a prefix derived from Greek meaning 'skin', as in
'dermatitis', 'dermatologist' and 'dermatology'.

determiner is a word used in front of a noun or pronoun to
tell us something about it. Unlike an adjective, it does not,
strictly speaking, 'describe' a noun or pronoun. **Determiners** are divided into the following categories—articles (a, an, the) as in 'a cat', 'an eagle', 'the book'; demonstrative determiners (this, that, these, those), as in
'this girl', 'that boy' and 'those people'; possessive determiners (my, your, his/her/its, our, their), as in 'my dog',
'her house', 'its colour', 'their responsibility'; numbers
(one ,two, three, four, etc, first, second, third, fourth, etc),
as in 'two reasons', 'five ways', 'ten children'; and indefinite or general determiners (all, another, any, both,
each, either, enough, every, few, fewer, less, little, many,
most, much, neither, no, other, several, some), as in 'both
parents', 'enough food', 'several issues'. Many words
used as determiners are also pronouns. *See* ADJECTIVE; DE-
MONSTRATIVE DETERMINER; POSSESSIVE DETERMINER; NUM-
BERS; INDEFINITE DETERMINER.

di- is a prefix derived from Greek meaning 'two' or 'double', as in 'dioxide', 'dilemma', 'diphthong' and 'disyllabic'.

dia- is a prefix meaning 'through', as in 'diaphanous';
'apart', as in 'diacritical', 'diaphragm' and 'dialysis'; and
'across', as in 'diameter'.

diacritic refers to a mark placed over, under or through a
letter to indicate a sound or stress value different from
that of the same letter when it is unmarked. **Diacritics** in-

clude the cedilla, as in 'façade', the German umlaut, as in 'mädchen' and diaeresis, as in 'naïve'.

diaeresis refers to a mark that is placed over a vowel to indicate that it is sounded separately from a neighbouring vowel, as in 'naïve', 'Chloë'.

dialect refers to a variety of language that is distinct from other varieties in terms of pronunciation, accent, vocabulary, grammar and sentence structure. The term **dialect** tends to imply a deviation from some standard form of language, usually the dialect used by educated upper-class or upper-middle-class people, known in English as 'standard' English.

Dialects may be regional in nature. Thus in Britain there is a Cornish dialect, a Liverpool dialect, a Glasgow dialect, and so on. Alternatively, they may be based on class differences, when they are sometimes known as 'social dialects'. These include working-class dialect, upper-class dialect, and so on.

At one time regional dialects were looked down on by people who spoke only standard English. People with regional accents, using regional dialects, were unlikely to get jobs in professions such as radio and television, where the use of language was a major consideration. People intent on such careers tried to change their accents to remove all traces of dialect. However, things have changed, and now it is quite common for people using regional accents and dialects to have jobs associated with radio and television.

Note that the word **dialect** is not appropriate if it is a global variety of English that is being referred to. For example, the

English spoken in America is known as American English.

diction has two meanings. It can refer to the choice of words in writing or speech, especially with regard to correctness, clarity or effectiveness, as in 'The content of his essay was very interesting but his diction was poor'. It can also refer to the pronunciation and enunciation of words in speaking and singing, as in 'She has a beautiful natural singing voice but should take lessons in diction'.

dialogue in novels, etc, is placed on a new line, often in a new paragraph, if there is a change of speaker, as in:

'We're going now', said John. 'Do you want to join us? If you do you'd better hurry. We can't wait.'

'Just go on', replied Mary. 'I'm not quite ready. I'll catch you up'.

digraph refers to a group of two letters representing one sound, as in 'ay' in 'hay', 'ey' in 'key', 'oy' in 'boy', 'ph' in 'phone' and 'th' in 'thin'. When the **digraph** consists of two letters physically joined together as 'ae', it is called a 'ligature'.

diminutive refers to something small or a small form or version of something, as in 'booklet', 'droplet', 'flatlet', 'auntie', 'doggy', 'islet', 'piglet', 'poppet', 'snippet', 'starlet', 'kitchenette', 'hillock', 'paddock', 'mannikin', 'lambkin', 'duckling', 'gosling', 'nestling', 'majorette', 'pipette'. Proper names often have diminutive forms. as in 'Alf' for Alfred, 'Annie' for Ann, 'Babs' for Barbara, 'Bill' for William, 'Charlie' for Charles, 'Dot' for Dorothy, 'Jimmy' for James, 'Lizzie' for Elizabeth, 'Meg' for Margaret, 'Nell' for Helen, 'Pat' for Patrick and 'Teddy' for Edward.

diphthong is a speech sound that changes its quality withi the same single syllable. The sound begins as for on vowel and moves on as for another. Since the sound glide from one vowel into another, a **diphthong** is sometime called a 'gliding vowel'. Examples include the vowe sounds in 'rain', 'weigh', 'either', 'voice', 'height 'aisle', 'road', 'soul', 'know', 'house', 'care', 'pure 'during', 'here' and 'weird'.

direct object refers to the noun, noun phrase, noun (nominal clause or pronoun which is acted upon by the ac tion of a transitive verb. In the sentence 'She bough milk', 'bought' is a transitive verb and 'milk' is a nou which is the direct object. In the sentence 'She bough loads of clothes', 'bought' is a transitive verb and 'load of clothes' is the direct object. In the sentence 'He know what happened', 'knows' is a transitive verb and 'wh: happened' is a 'noun clause' or 'nominal clause'. A **dire object** is frequently known just as 'object'. *See* INDIREC OBJECT.

direct speech refers to the reporting of speech by repeatin exactly the actual words used by the speaker. In the ser tence 'Peter said, "I am tired of this"', "I am tired of this is a piece of direct speech because it represents exactl what Peter said. Similarly, in the sentence 'Jane askec "Where are you going?"', "Where are you going" is piece of direct speech since it represents exactly wh: Jane said.

Quotation marks, also known as inverted commas or i formally as quotes, are used at the beginning and the en of pieces of **direct speech.** Only the words actually sp ken are placed within the quotation marks, as in '"If I were you," he said, "I would refuse to go"'. The quotation marks involved can be either single or double, according to preference or house style.

If there is a statement such as 'he said' following the piece of direct speech, a comma is placed before the second inverted comma, as in '"Come along," he said'. If the piece of direct speech is a question or exclamation, a question mark or exclamation mark is put instead of the comma, as in '"What are you doing?" asked John' and '"Get away from me!" she screamed'.

If a statement such as 'he said' is placed within a sentence in direct speech, a comma is placed after 'he said' and the second part of the piece of direct speech does not begin with a capital letter, as in '"I know very well," he said, "that you do not like me."'

If the piece of direct speech includes a complete sentence, the sentence begins with a capital letter, as in '"I am going away," she said, "and I am not coming back. I don't feel that I belong here anymore."' Note that the full stop at the end of a piece of direct speech that is a sentence should go before the closing inverted comma.

If the piece of direct speech quoted takes up more than one paragraph, quotation marks are placed at the beginning of each new paragraph. However, quotation marks are not placed at the end of each paragraph, just at the end of the final one.

When writing a story, etc, which includes dialogue or conversation, each new piece of direct speech should begin on a new line or sometimes in a new paragraph.

Quotation marks are not used only to indicate **direct speech.** For example, they are sometimes used to indicate the title of a book or newspaper. The quotation mark used in this way can be either single or double, according to preference or house style. If a piece of direct speech contains the title of a book, newspaper, etc, it should be put in the opposite type of quotation marks to those used to enclose the piece of direct speech. Thus, if single quotation marks have been used in the direct speech, then double quotation marks should be used for the title within the direct speech, as in ''Have you read "Animal Farm" by George Orwell?' the teacher asked'. If double quotation marks have been used for the direct speech, single quotation marks should be used for the title, as in '"Have you read 'Animal Farm?' by George Orwell?" the teacher asked'.

Sometimes titles are put in italic type instead of quotation marks. This avoids the clumsiness which can occur when both sets of quotation marks end on the same word, as in 'The pupil replied, 'No, I have not read "Animal Farm".''

dis- is a prefix derived from Latin indicating 'opposite' 'not', as in 'disappear', 'disapprove', 'disband', 'disbelieve', 'disclaim', 'disconnect', 'discontinue', 'disenchant', 'disengage', 'disinherit', 'dislike', 'disobey', 'dispossess', 'distrust', and 'disunite'.

distributive pronouns refer to individual members of a class or group. These include 'each', 'either', 'neither' 'none', 'everyone', 'no one'. Such pronouns, where relevant, should be accompanied by singular verbs and sin gular personal pronouns, as in 'All the men are to be considered for the new posts. Each is to send in his application'. Problems arise when the sex of the noun to which the **distributive pronoun** refers back is either unknown or unspecified. Formerly it was the convention to treat such nouns as masculine and so to make the **distributive pronoun** masculine, as in 'All pupils must obey the rules. Each is to provide his own sports equipment'. Nowadays this convention is frequently considered to be unacceptably sexist and attempts have been made to get round this. One solution is to use 'him/her' (or 'him or her'), etc, as in 'The students have received a directive from the professor. Each is to produce his/her essay by tomorrow.' This convention is considered by many people to be clumsy. They prefer to be ungrammatical and use a plural personal pronoun, as in 'The pupils are being punished. Each is to inform their parents'. Where possible it is preferable to rephrase sentences to avoid being either sexist or ungrammatical, as in 'All of the pupils must tell their parents.'

Each, either, etc, in such contexts is fairly formal. In less formal situations 'each of', 'either of', etc, is more usual, as in 'Each of the boys will have to train really hard to win' and 'Either of the dresses is perfectly suitable'.

isyllabic means having two syllable. For example 'window' is disyllabic, since it consists of the syllable 'win' and the syllable 'dow'. Similarly 'curtain' is disyllabic since it consists of the syllable 'cur' and 'tain'.

o is an auxiliary verb which is used to form negative forms, as in, 'I do not agree with you', 'They do not always win', 'He does not wish to go' and 'She did not approve of their behaviour'. It is also used to form interrogative forms, as in 'Do you agree?', 'Does she know about it?', 'Did you see that?' and 'I prefer to go by train Don't you?' **Do** is also used for emphasis, as in 'I do believe you're right' and 'They do know, don't they?'

-dom is a suffix meaning 'state, condition', as in 'boredom', 'freedom', 'officialdom', 'martyrdom'. It can also mean 'rank or status', as in 'earldom', 'dukedom', or 'domain, territory' as in 'kingdom'.

double negative refers to the occurrence of two negative words in a single sentence or clause, as in 'He didn't say nothing' and 'We never had no quarrel'. This is usually considered incorrect in standard English, although it is a feature of some social or regional dialects. The use of the **double negative**, if taken literally, often has the opposite meaning to the one intended. Thus 'He didn't say nothing' conveys the idea that 'He said something'.

Some **double negatives** are considered acceptable, as in 'I wouldn't be surprised if they don't turn up', although it is better to restrict such constructions to informal contexts. The sentence quoted conveys the impression that the speaker will be quite surprised if 'they' do 'turn up' Another example of an acceptable **double negative** is 'I can't not worry about the children. Anything could have happened to them'. Again this type of construction is best restricted to informal contexts.

It is the semi-negative forms, such as 'hardly' and 'scarcely', which cause most problems with regard to **double negatives**, as in 'We didn't have hardly any money to buy food' and 'They didn't have barely enough time to catch the bus'. Such sentences are incorrect.

double passive refers to a clause which contains two verbs in the passive, the second of which is an infinitive, as in 'The goods are expected to be despatched some time this week'. Some examples of **double passives** are clumsy or ungrammatical and should be avoided, as in 'Redundancy notices are proposed to be issued next week'.

doubling of consonants causes spelling problems. There are a few rules which help to solve these problems. These include the following: In words of one syllable ending in a single consonant preceded by a single vowel, the consonant is doubled when an ending starting with a vowel is added, as in 'drop' and 'dropped', 'pat' and 'patting' and 'rub' and 'rubbing'.

In words of more than one syllable that end in a single consonant preceded by a single vowel, the consonant is doubled if the stress is on the last syllable, as in 'begin' and 'beginning', 'occur' and 'occurring', 'prefer' and 'preferred', 'refer' and 'referring' and 'commit' and 'committed'. In similar words where the stress is not on the last syllable, the consonant does not double, as in 'bigot' and 'bigoted' and 'develop' and 'developed'.

Exceptions to this rule include words ending in 'l'. The 'l' doubles even in cases where the last syllable containing it is unstressed, as in 'travel' and 'travelled' and 'appal' and 'appalling'. 'Worship', in which the stress is on the first syllable, is also an exception, as in 'worshipped'.

doubles are words that habitually go together, as in 'out and out', 'neck and neck', 'over and over', 'hale and hearty', 'rant and rave', 'fast and furious', 'hue and cry', 'stuff and nonsense', 'rough and ready', 'might and main', 'give and take', 'ups and downs', 'fair and square', 'high and dry' and 'wear and tear'. **Doubles** are also sometimes called **dyads**.

doublets are pairs of words that have developed from the same original word but now differ somewhat in form and usually in meaning. Examples include 'human' and 'humane', 'shade' and 'shadow', 'hostel' and 'hotel', 'frail' and 'fragile', and 'fashion' and 'faction'.

dramatic irony refers to a situation in which a character in a play, novel, etc, says or does something that has a meaning for the audience or reader, other than the obvious meaning, that he/she does not understand. Its use is common in both comedy and tragedy.

dual gender refers to a category of nouns in which there is no indication of gender. The nouns referred to include a range of words used for people, and occasionally animals, which can be of either gender. Unless the gender is specified we do not know the sex of the person referred to. Such words include 'artist', 'author', 'poet', 'singer', 'child', 'pupil', 'student', 'baby', 'parent', 'teacher', 'dog'. Such words give rise to problems with accompanying singular pronouns. *See* EACH.

dummy subject describes a subject that has no intrinsic meaning but is inserted to maintain a balanced grammatical structure. In the sentences 'It has started to rain' and 'It is nearly midnight', 'it' is a dummy subject. In the sentences 'There is nothing else to say' and 'There is no reason for his behaviour', 'there' is a dummy subject.

yads see **doubles**.

ynamic verb refers to a verb with a meaning that indicates action, as 'work' in 'They work hard', 'play' in 'The boys play football at the weekend' and 'come' in 'The girls come here every Sunday'.

ys- is a prefix derived from the Greek meaning 'bad', as in 'dyslexia', 'dysgraphia', 'dysmenorrhea', 'dyspepsia'.

E

each can be either a DETERMINER or a DISTRIBUTIVE PRONOUN. **Each** as a determiner is used before a singular noun and is accompanied by a singular verb, as in 'Each candidate is to reapply', 'Each athlete has a place in the final', 'Each country is represented by a head of state' and 'Each cha[ir] was covered in chintz'.

Each of can sometimes be used instead of **each**, as in 'each of the candidates'. Again a singular verb is used, a[s] in 'Each of the books has pages missing', 'Each of th[e] chairs has a broken leg' and 'Each of the pupils is to mak[e] a contribution to the cost of the outing'. **Each of** can als[o] be used in front of plural pronouns, as in 'each of them'. Once again a singular verb is used, as in 'Each of the[m] wants something different', 'Each of us is supposed [to] make a contribution' and 'Each of the words has sever[al] meanings'. If the user wishes to emphasize the fact th[at] something is true about every member of a group, **eac[h] one of** should be used and not 'every', as in 'Each one o[f] them feels guilty', 'Each one of us has a part to play' an[d] 'Each one of the actors has improved'.

As a pronoun **each** also takes a singular verb, as [in] 'They hate each other. Each is plotting revenge', 'The[se] exercises are not a waste of time. Each provides valuab[le] experience'. For emphasis **each one** can be used, as in 'We cannot leave any of these books behind. Each one of them is necessary' and 'We should not dismiss any of the staff. Each one has a part to play in the new firm'.

Each, where relevant, should be accompanied by a singular personal pronoun, as in 'Each girl has to provide her own sports equipment', 'Each of the men is to take a turn at working night shift', 'The boys are all well off and each can afford the cost of the holiday' and 'There are to be no exceptions among the women staff. Each one has to work full time'.

Problems arise when the noun that **each** refers back to is of unknown or unspecified sex. Formerly nouns in such situations were assumed to be masculine, as in 'Each pupil was required to bring his own tennis racket' and 'Each of the students has to provide himself with a tape recorder'. Nowadays such a convention is regarded as being sexist and the use of 'he/her', 'his/her', etc, is proposed, as in 'Each pupil was required to bring his/her (or 'his or her') own tennis racket' and 'Each student has to provide himself/herself (or 'himself or herself') with a tape recorder'. Even in written English such a convention can be clumsy and it is even more so in spoken English. For this reason many people decide to be ungrammatical and opt for 'Each pupil was required to bring their own tennis racket' and 'Each student has to provide themselves with a tape recorder'.

Both sexism and grammatical error can be avoided by rephrasing such sentences, as in 'All pupils are required to bring their own tennis rackets' and 'All students have to provide themselves with tape recorders'.

Each is used rather than **every** when the user is thinking of the members of a group as individuals.

eco- is a prefix indicating ecology. Following the increase awareness of the importance of the environment, ther has been a growing interest in ecology and many word beginning with **eco-** have been added to the English lan guage. Some of these are scientific terms such a 'ecotype', 'ecosystem' or 'ecospecies'. Others are mor general terms, such as 'ecocatastrophe' and 'ecopolitics' and some are even slang terms, such as 'ecofreak' an 'econut'.

-ectomy is a suffix of Greek origin which indicates 'surgi cal removal', as in 'hysterectomy', the surgical remova of the womb, 'mastectomy', the surgical removal of breast, and 'appendicectomy', the surgical removal of th appendix, the American English version of which is 'ap pendectomy'.

-ed is a suffix which forms the past tense and past partici ples of regular verbs, as in 'asked', 'blinded', 'caused 'darkened', 'escaped', 'frightened', 'guarded', 'hunted 'injured', 'jilted', 'kicked', 'landed', 'marked', 'noted 'opened', 'painted', 'quarrelled', 'rattled', 'started', 'tor mented', 'unveiled', 'washed', 'yielded'. Some past part ciples ending in '-ed' can act as adjectives, as in 'dark ened room', 'escaped prisoners', 'frightened children 'hunted animals', 'painted faces' and 'tormented souls'.

In the case of some verbs, the past tense and past partic ple may end in '-ed' or 't', according to preference. Suc verbs include 'burn', 'dream', 'dwell', 'kneel', 'lean 'leapt', 'smell', 'spell', 'spill' and 'spoil'. Thus 'burned' and 'burnt', 'dreamed' and 'dreamt', 'kneeled' and 'knelt', and 'learned' and 'learnt', etc, are acceptable forms.

-ee is a suffix derived from French and is used as part of nouns that are the recipients of an action, as in 'deportee', a person who has been deported; 'employee', a person who is employed; 'interviewee', a person who is being interviewed; 'licensee', a person who has been licensed; 'trainee', a person who is being trained.

   -Ee can also be used as part of a noun indicating a person who acts or behaves in a particular way, as 'absentee', a person who absents himself/herself and 'escapee', a person who escapes.

e.g. is the abbreviation of the Latin phrase *exempli gratia* and means 'for example'. It is used before examples of what has previously been referred to, as in 'The tourists want to visit the historic sites of Edinburgh, e.g. Edinburgh Castle and Holyrood House'. By its very nature e.g. is mostly restricted to written English, becoming 'for example' in speech. Many writers also prefer to use 'for example' rather than use e.g. Both letters of the abbreviation usually have a full stop after them, as e.g., and it is usually preceded by a comma.

either can be used as either a determiner or distributive pronoun. As a determiner it is used with a singular verb, as in 'Either hotel is expensive' and 'In principle they are both against the plan but is either likely to vote for it?'

   Either of can be used instead of **either**. It is used before a plural noun, as in 'either of the applicants' and 'either of the houses'. It is accompanied by a singular verb, as in 'Either of the applicants is suitable' and 'Either of the houses is big enough for their family'.

Either can be used as a distributive pronoun and takes a singular verb, as in 'We have looked at both houses and either is suitable' and 'She cannot decide between the two dresses but either is appropriate for the occasion'. This use is rather formal.

In the **either .... or** construction, a singular verb is used if both subjects are singular, as in 'Either Mary or Jane knows what to do' and 'Either my mother or my father plans to be present'. A plural verb is used if both nouns involved are plural, as in 'Either men or women can play' and 'Either houses or flats are available'.

When a combination of singular and plural subjects is involved, the verb traditionally agrees with the subject which is nearer to it, as in 'Either his parents or his sister is going to come' and 'Either his grandmother or his parents are going to come'.

As a pronoun, **either** should be used only of two possibilities.

electro- is a prefix meaning 'electric, electrical' as in 'electrocardiograph', 'electromagnetic', 'electroscope', 'electrotherapy'.

elision refers to the omission of a speech sound or syllable as in the omission of 'd' in one of the possible pronunciations of 'Wednesday' and in the omission of 'ce' from the pronunciation of 'Gloucester'.

ellipsis indicates omission of some kind. It can refer to the omission of words from a statement because they are thought to be obvious from the context. In many cases it involves using an auxiliary verb on its own rather than a full verb, as in 'Jane won't accept it but Mary will' and 'They would go if they could'. In such cases the full form of 'Jane won't accept it but Mary will accept it' and 'They would go if they could go' would sound unnatural and repetitive. This is common in spoken English. Some sentences containing an ellipsis sound clumsy as well as ungrammatical, as in 'This is as good, or perhaps even better than that', where 'as' is omittedafter 'good' and in 'People have and still do express their disapproval about it', where 'expressed' is omitted after 'have'. Care should be taken to avoid ellipsis if the use of it is going to be ambiguous or clumsy.

Ellipsis is often used to indicate an omission from a quoted passage. If part of a passage is quoted and there is a gap before the next piece of the same passage is required to be quoted an **ellipsis** is used in the form of three dots. If the part of the passage quoted does not start at the beginning of a sentence the ellipsis precedes it.

emphasizing adjective is an adjective used for emphasis. 'Very' is an **emphasizing adjective** in the sentence 'His very mother dislikes him' and 'own' is an **emphasizing adjective** in 'He likes to think that he is own master'.

emphasizing adverb is an adverb used for emphasis. 'Really' is an **emphasizing adverb** in the sentence 'She really doesn't care whether she lives or dies' and 'positively' is an **emphasizing adverb** in the sentence 'He positively does not want to know anything about it'.

emphatic pronoun is a reflexive pronoun that is used for

emphasis, as in 'He knows himself that he is wrong', 'Sh
admitted herself that she had made a mistake' and 'Th
teachers themselves say that the headmaster is too strict'

-en is a suffix with several functions. In one sense it indi
cates 'causing to be', as in 'broaden', 'darken', 'gladden'
'lighten' and 'sweeten'. It also indicates a diminutive o
small version of something, as in 'chicken' and 'maiden'
It also indicates what something is made of, as in 'silken'
'wooden' and 'woollen'. It is also used to form the pas
participle of many irregular words, as 'broken', 'fallen'
'forgotten' and 'taken'.

en- is a prefix indicating 'causing to be', as in 'enrich' and
'enlarge', and 'putting into', as in 'endanger', 'enrage'
'enslave'.

ending is the final part of a word consisting of an inflectior
which is added to a base or root word. The '-ren' part o
'children' is an ending, the '-er' of 'poorer' is an ending
and the '-ing' of 'falling' is an ending.

epic originally referred to a very long narrative poem deal
ing with heroic deeds and adventures on a grand scale, a
Homer's 'Iliad'. In modern usage it has been extended to
include novels or films with some of these qualities.

epigram is a figure of speech consisting of a brief, pointe
and witty saying, as in Jonathan Swift's 'Every man de
sires to live long; but no man would be old' and Osca
Wilde's 'A cynic is a man who knows the price of every
thing and the value of nothing'. **Epigram** originally re
ferred to a short poem inscribed on a public monument o
tomb.

epithet is an adjective that describes a quality of a noun, a in 'a beautiful dress', 'an amazing story' and 'an enjoyable occasion'. It is also used to indicate a term of abuse, as in 'The drunk man let out a stream of epithets at the policeman.'

eponym refers to a person after whom something is named. The name of the thing in question can also be referred to as an eponym, or it can be said to be eponymous, eponymous being the adjective from **eponym**. English has several eponymous words. Some of these are listed below together with their derivations.

Bailey bridge, a type of temporary military bridge that can be assembled very quickly, called after Sir Donald **Bailey** (1901-85), the English engineer who invented it.

Bowie knife, a type of hunting knife with a long curving blade, called after the American soldier and adventurer, James **Bowie** (1799-1836), who made it popular.

cardigan, a knitted jacket fastened with buttons called after the Earl of **Cardigan** (1797-1868) who was fond of wearing such a garment and was the British cavalry officer who led the unsuccessful Charge of the Light Brigade during the Crimean War (1854).

Celsius the temperature scale, called after the Swedish astronomer, Anders **Celsius** (1701-44).

freesia, a type of sweet-smelling flower, called after the German physician, Friedrich Heinrich Theodor **Freese** (died 1876).

garibaldi, a type of biscuit with a layer of currants in it, called after Giuseppe **Garibaldi** (1807-1882), an Italian soldier patriot who is said to have enjoyed such biscuits.

Granny Smith, a variety of hard green apple, called after the Australian gardener, Maria Ann Smith, known as **Granny Smith** (died 1870), who first grew the apple in Sydney in the 1860s.

greengage, a type of greenish plum, called after Sir William **Gage** who introduced it into Britain from France (1777-1864).

leotard, a one-piece, close-fitting garment worn by acrobats and dancers, called after the French acrobat, Jules **Leotard** (1842-70), who introduced the costume as a circus garment.

mackintosh, a type of raincoat, especially one made of rubberized cloth, called after the Scottish chemist, Charles **Mackintosh** (1766-1843), who patented it in the early 1820s.

praline, a type of confectionery made from nuts and sugar, is called after Count Plessis-**Praslin** (1598-1675), a French field marshal, whose chef is said to have been the first person to make the sweet.

plimsoll, a type of light rubber-soled canvas shoe, called after the English shipping reform leader, Samuel **Plimsoll** (1824-98). The shoe is so named because the upper edge of the rubber was thought to resemble the **Plimsoll** Line, the set of markings on the side of a ship which indicate the levels to which the ship may be safely loaded. The Plimsoll Line became law in 1876.

salmonella, the bacteria that causes some diseases such as food poisoning, called after Daniel Elmer **Salmon** (1850-1914), the American veterinary surgeon who identified it.

sandwich, a snack consisting of two pieces of buttered

bread with a filling, called after the Earl of **Sandwich** (1718-92) who was such a compulsive gambler that he would not leave the gaming tables to eat, but had some cold beef between two slices of bread brought to him.

saxophone, a type of keyed brass instrument often used in jazz music, called after Adolphe **Sax** (1814-94), the Belgium instrument-maker who invented it.

shrapnel, an explosive projectile that contains bullets or fragments of metal and a charge that is exploded before impact, called after the British army officer, Henry **Shrapnel** (1761–1842), who invented it.

stetson, a type of wide-brimmed, high-crowned felt hat, called after its designer, the American hat-maker, John Batterson **Stetson** (1830-1906).

trilby, a type of soft felt hat with an indented crown, called after 'Trilby', the dramatized version of the novel by the English writer, George du Maurier. The heroine of the play, Trilby O'Ferrall, wore such a hat.

wellington, a waterproof rubber boot that extends to the knee, called after the Duke of **Wellington** (1769-1852), who defeated Napoleon at Waterloo (1815).

equative indicates that one thing is equal to, or the same as, another. The verb 'to be' is sometimes known as an **equative verb** because it links a subject and complement which are equal to each other, as in 'He is a rogue' ('he' and 'rogue' refer to the same person) and 'His wife is a journalist' ('his wife' and 'journalist' refer to the same person). Other **equative verbs** include 'appear', 'become', 'look', 'remain' and 'seem', as in 'She looks a nasty person' and 'He became a rich man'. Such verbs are more usually known as **copular verbs**.

-er is a suffix with several functions. It can indicate 'a person that does something', as in 'bearer', 'cleaner', 'employer', 'farmer', 'manager'. Some words in this category can also end in '-or', as in 'adviser/advisor'. It can also indicate 'a person who is engaged in something', as in 'lawyer'. It also indicates 'a thing which does something', as in 'blender', 'cooker', 'mower', 'printer' and 'strainer'. It can also indicate the comparative form of an adjective, as in 'darker', 'fairer', 'older', 'shorter' and 'younger'. It can also indicate 'someone that comes from somewhere', as in 'Londoner' and 'Southerner'.

-esque is a prefix of French origin which means 'in the style or fashion of', as in 'Junoesque', 'statuesque', 'Picassoesque', 'Ramboesque'.

-ese is a suffix indicating 'belonging to, coming from' and is used of people and languages, as 'Chinese', 'Japanese' and 'Portuguese'. By extension it refers to words indicating some kind of jargon, as 'computerese', 'journalese' and 'officialese'.

Esq. can be used instead of 'Mr' when addressing an envelope to a man, as in 'John Jones, Esq.'. It is mostly used in formal contexts. Note that Esq. is used instead of 'Mr', not as well as it. It is usually spelt with a full stop.

-ess is a suffix which was formerly widely used to indicate the feminine form of a word, as 'authoress' from 'author', 'poetess' from 'poet', 'editress' from 'editor', and 'sculptress' from 'sculptor'. In many cases the supposed male form, such as 'author', is now considered a neutral form and so is used of both a woman and a man. Thus a woman

as well as a man may be an author, a poet, an editor and a
sculptor, etc. Some words ending in **-ess** remain, as princess, duchess, heiress and hostess. Actress and waitress
are still also fairly widespread.

-est is a suffix which indicates the superlative forms of adjectives, as in 'biggest', 'hardest', 'lowest', 'smallest',
'ugliest'.

etc is the abbreviation of a Latin phrase *et cetera*, meaning
'and the rest, and other things'. It is used at the end of lists
to indicate that there exist other examples of the kind of
thing that has just been named, as in 'He grows potatoes,
carrots, turnips, etc', 'The girls can play tennis, hockey,
squash, etc', 'The main branch of the bank can supply
francs, marks, lire, kroner, etc'. **Etc** is preceded by a
comma and is also spelt with a full stop.

-ette is a suffix indicating a diminutive or smaller version,
as 'cigarette', 'kitchenette', 'rosette', 'serviette'. It can
also indicate 'imitation', as in 'flannelette', 'leatherette',
'satinette'. It can also indicate 'female', as in 'majorette',
'usherette', 'suffragette'. In this last sense it is sometimes
used disparagingly, as in 'jockette' (a derogatory word for
a female jockey) and 'hackette' (a derogatory word for a
female journalist).

etymology refers to the source of the formation of a word
and the development of its meaning, as in 'What is the
etymology of the word "biochemistry"?' It also means the
branch of language studies that deals with the origin and
development of words, as in 'He specializes in etymology'. In addition it refers to an account or statement of the
formation of a word or phrase, as in 'Does that dictionary

have etymologies?' In larger dictionaries it is usual to include etymologies, often at the end of each entry. These indicate which language the relevant word has been derived from, for example, whether it has come from Old English, Norse, Latin, Greek, French, German, Dutch, Italian, Spanish, etc. Alternatively they indicate which person, place, etc, the word has been named after. Some dictionaries also include the date at which the relevant word entered the English language. *See* BORROWING.

Many words and phrases in the English language are of unknown or uncertain origin. In such cases much guesswork goes on and various suggestions put forward, most of which cannot be proved.

euphemism is a term given to an expression that is a milder, more pleasant, less direct way of saying something that might be thought to be too harsh or direct. English has a great many euphemisms, many of these referring to certain areas of life. Euphemisms range from the high-flown, to the coy, to slang. Some examples of euphemisms and of the areas in which they tend to occur are listed below.

euphemisms for 'die' or 'be dead':
'be in the arms of Jesus', 'be laid to rest', 'be with one's maker', 'be no longer with us', 'be with the Lord', 'be written out of the script', 'bite the dust', 'cash in one's chips', 'croak', 'depart this life', 'go to a better place', 'go the way of all flesh', 'go to one's long home', 'go to the happy hunting grounds', 'have been taken by the grim reaper', 'have bought it', 'have breathed one's last', 'have gone to a better place', 'kick the bucket', 'meet one's

end', 'pass away', 'pay the supreme sacrifice', 'pop off', 'push up the daisies', 'rest in peace', 'shuffle off this mortal coil', 'slip one's rope', 'turn up one's toes'.

euphemisms for 'old':
'getting on a bit', 'not as young as one was', 'not in the first flush of youth', 'in the sunset years', 'in the twilight years', 'of advanced years', 'so many years young (as in 90 years young)'.

euphemisms for 'suicide':
'do away with one self', 'die by one's own hand', 'end it all', 'make away with oneself', 'take one's own life', 'take the easy way out', 'top oneself'.

euphemisms for 'to dismiss':
'declare (someone) redundant', 'deselect', 'dispense with (someone's) services', 'give early retirement to', 'give (someone) a golden handshake', 'give (someone) his/her marching orders', 'let (someone) go', 'not to renew (someone's) contract'.

euphemisms for 'drunk':
'blotto', 'feeling no pain ', 'happy', 'half-cut', 'legless', 'merry', 'one over the eight', 'plastered', 'three sheets to the wind', 'tiddly', 'tipsy', 'tired and emotional', 'squiffy', 'well-oiled'.

euphemisms for 'naked':
'in a state of nature', 'in one's birthday suit', 'in the buff', 'in the nuddy', 'in the raw', 'starkers', 'without a stitch', 'wearing only a smile'.

euphemisms for 'pregnant':
'awaiting the patter of tiny feet', 'expecting', 'expecting a happy event', 'in a delicate condition', 'in an interesting

condition', 'in the club', 'in the family way', 'in the pudding club', 'up the pole', 'up the spout', 'with a bun in the oven'.

euphemisms for 'to have sexual intercourse':
'be intimate with', 'do it', 'get one's end away', 'go to bed with', 'have it off with', 'make love', 'make out', 'sleep with', 'score'.

euphemisms for 'sexual intercourse':
'hanky panky', 'intimacy', 'nookie', 'roll in the hay', 'rumpy pumpy/rumpty pumpty'.

euphemisms for to go to the toilet:
'answer the call of nature', 'freshen up', 'go somewhere', 'pay a visit', 'powder one's nose', 'spend a penny', 'take a slash', 'wash one's hands'.

euphemisms for 'toilet':
'bathroom', 'bog', 'can', 'john', 'karzy', 'powder room', 'rest room', 'the facilities', 'the conveniences', 'the geography of the house', 'the little boys' room/the little girls room', 'the littlest room', 'the smallest room', 'the plumbing', 'wash room'.

euphemisms and political correctness:
Many of the expressions advocated by the politically correct movement for viewing physical and mental disabilities in a more positive light are in fact **euphemisms** These include 'aurally challenged' for 'deaf', 'optically challenged' for 'blind', and 'uniquely abled' for 'physically disabled'.

Euro- is a prefix meaning either 'referring to Europe', as in 'Eurovision', but more commonly now 'referring to the European Community', as in 'Euro-MP', 'Eurocrat' 'Eurocurrency'.

every is used with a singular noun to indicate that all the members of a group are being referred to. It takes a singular verb, as in 'Every soldier must report for duty', 'Every machine is to be inspected' and 'Every house has a different view'. **Every** should also be accompanied, where relevant, by a singular pronoun, as in 'Every boy has his job to do', 'Every girl is to wear a dress' and 'Every machine is to be replaced'. Problems arise when the sex of the noun to which **every** refers is unknown or unspecified. Formerly it was the custom to assume such a noun to be masculine and to use masculine pronouns, as in 'Every pupil is to behave himself properly. This assumption is now regarded as sexist, and to avoid this 'he/she', 'him/her' and 'his/her' can be used. Many people feel that this convention can become clumsy and prefer to be ungrammatical by using 'they', 'them' and 'their', as in 'Every pupil is to behave themselves properly.' Many sentences of this kind can be rephrased to avoid being either sexist or ungrammatical, as in 'All pupils are to behave themselves properly'. *See* EACH.

everyone is a pronoun which takes a singular verb, as in 'Everyone is welcome' and 'Everyone has the right to a decent standard of living'. In order to be grammatically correct, it should be accompanied, where relevant, by a singular personal pronoun but it is subject to the same kind of treatment as **every**. *See* EVERY.

ex- is a prefix meaning 'former', as in 'ex-chairman', 'ex-president', 'ex-wife'.

exclamation is a word, phrase or sentence called out with strong feeling of some kind. It is marked by an **exclama-**

tion mark which occurs at the end of the **exclamation**, as in 'Get lost!', 'What a nerve!', 'Help!', 'Ouch!' 'Well I never!', 'What a disaster!', 'I'm tired of all this!' and 'Let me out of here!' An **exclamatory question** is a sentence that is interrogative in form but is an **exclamation** in meaning, as in 'Isn't the baby beautiful!' and 'Isn't it lovely!'.

extra-is a prefix meaning 'beyond, outside' as in 'extra-marital', 'extra-terrestrial', 'extra-curricular'.

F

fable is a story that is intended to convey a moral lesson. **Fables** frequently feature animals which speak and act like human beings. Most famous are those of Aesop, a Phrygian slave (620–560 BC), who wrote such fables as 'The Hare and the Tortoise' and 'The Fox and the Grapes'.

false friends refer to words that have the same or similar forms in different languages but have different meanings in each. For example, the French word *abusif* and the English word 'abusive' are **false friends**. *Abusif* does not mean 'abusive' but 'incorrect, illegal, unauthorized, excessive'. Similarly, the French word *actuel* and the English 'actual' are **false friends**. *Actuel* does not mean 'actual' but 'present-day'. Similarly, the French *eventuel* and Italian *eventuale* are false freinds with the English 'eventual'. *Eventuel* and *eventuale* do not mean 'eventual' but 'possible', while *sensible* in French and *sensibile* in Italian do not mean 'sensible, having good sense or judgement' but 'sensitive, tender, touchy'.

feminine refers to the gender that indicates female persons or animals. It is the opposite of 'masculine'. The feminine gender demands the use of the appropriate pronoun, including 'she', 'her', 'hers' and 'herself', as in 'The girl tried to save the dog but *she* was unable to do so', 'The woman hurt *her* leg', 'Mary said that the book is *hers*', and 'The waitress cut *herself*'.

feminine forms of words, formed by adding —*ess*, used to be common but many such forms are now thought to be sexist. Words such as 'author', 'sculptor', 'poet' are now considered to be neutral terms that can be used to refer to a man or a woman. Some -*ess* words are either still being used or are in a state of flux, as in 'actress'. See -ESS.

few and **a few** are not interchangeable. Both expressions mean 'some, but not many', but they convey different impressions. **Few** is the opposite of 'many', as in 'We have few resources' and 'We have few ideas left'. **A few** conveys a more positive impression and is the opposite of 'none', as in 'We have a few pounds set aside for Christmas' and 'We have not reached a definite decision but we have a few ideas in hand'. The sentence 'We have few ideas left' indicates a negative situation, that 'we' are running out of 'ideas', but the sentence 'We have a few ideas in hand' conveys a positive impression.

fewer and **less** are liable to be used wrongly. **Fewer** means 'a smaller number of' and should be used with plural nouns, as in 'fewer problems', 'fewer resources', 'fewer fears', 'fewer boxes', 'fewer books', 'fewer bottles' and 'fewer chairs'. **Less** means 'a smaller amount of' and should be used with singular nouns, as in 'less responsibility', less anxiety', less work', 'less milk', 'less wood' and 'less material'. It is a very common error to use **less** where **fewer** is correct, as in 'less bottles' and 'less queues'.

figurative refers to words that are not used literally. For example, 'mine' in the sense of 'excavation in the earth from which coal, tin, etc, is taken' is a literal use of the word. 'Mine' in the sense of 'He is a mine of information' is a figurative use of the word. There are many figurative expressions in English. These include 'take the bull by the horns', 'put one's shoulder to the wheel', 'hide one's light under a bushel', 'be in seventh heaven', 'count one's chickens', 'change horses in mid-stream', 'blow hot and cold', 'run with the hare and hunt with the hounds', 'make the feathers fly', 'put the cat among the pigeons', 'cut corners', 'cry over spilt milk', 'jump on the bandwagon', 'let the grass grow under one's feet', 'drop a brick', 'burn the midnight oil', 'show a clean pair of heels', 'turn one's coat', 'drive a coach and horses through' and 'take coals to Newcastle'.

figure of speech is a form of expression used to heighten the effect of a statement. The most commonly known are 'similes' and 'metaphors' but there are many more, such as 'personification'. See the individual entries for further information.

finite verb is a verb that has a tense and has a subject with which it agrees in number and person. For example 'cries' is finite in the sentence 'The child cries most of the time', and 'looks' is finite in the sentence 'The old man looks ill'. However 'go' in the sentence 'He wants to go' is non-finite since it has no variation of tense and does not have a subject. Similarly in the sentence 'Sitting on the river-bank, he was lost in thought', 'sitting' is non-finite.

finite clause is a clause which contains a 'finite verb', as in 'when she sees him', 'after she had defeated him', and 'as they were sitting there'.

first person refers to the person who is speaking or writing when referring to himself or herself. The **first person** pronouns are 'I', 'me', 'myself' and 'mine', with the plural forms being 'we', 'us', 'ourselves' and 'ours'. Examples include 'She said, "*I* am going home"', '"*I* am going shopping," he said', '"*We* have very little money left," she said to her husband' and 'He said, "*We* shall have to leave now if we are to get there on time"'. The first person determiners are 'my' and 'our', as in 'I have forgotten to bring *my* notebook' and 'We must remember to bring *our* books home.'

fixed phrase, also called **set phrase**, refers to a phrase that has no, or virtually no, variants, as in 'from bad to worse', 'to and fro', 'hither and thither', 'horse and cart', 'this and that', 'alas and alack' and 'rough and ready'.

-fold is a suffix meaning 'times, multiplied by', as in fourfold, a hundredfold.

for- is a prefix derived from Old English with several meanings. These include 'prohibition', as in 'forbid'; 'abstention' as in 'forbear', 'forgo' and 'forswear'; 'neglect', as in 'forsake'; 'excess, intensity', as in 'forlorn'; and 'away, off, apart', as in 'forgive'.

fore- is a prefix derived from Old English meaning 'before', as in 'forecast', 'forestall', 'foretell', 'forewarn', 'foregoing' and 'forefathers'. It can also mean 'front', as in 'foreleg', 'forehead', 'forepart'.

foreign plural refers to a plural of a word in English that has retained the plural form of the foreign word from which the English word has been derived. Examples include 'phenomena' from 'phenomenon', 'crises' from 'crisis' and 'criteria' from 'criterion'. There is a modern tendency to anglicize some of the foreign plural forms. In some cases the foreign plural form and the anglicized form exist alongside each other as 'formulae/formulas', 'thesauri/thesauruses', 'radii/radiuses', 'indices/indexes' and 'bureaux/bureaus'.

foreign expressions which have been adopted into English but not 'naturalized' are sometimes written in italic type, as in *bête noire* (a fear or obsession), *rara avis* (a rarity), *en passant* (in passing), *hors de combat*, (out of the contest, disabled), *en route* (on the way), *bon mot* (witty saying), *in toto* (completely), *in flagrante delicto* (in the very act of committing an offence), *enfant terrible* (a person who causes embarrassment by indiscreet or outrageous behaviour), *en famille* (with one's family) and *inter alia* (among other things).

-form is a suffix meaning 'having the form of', as in 'cruciform', or 'having such a number of', as in 'uniform', 'multiform'.

formal refers to speech and writing that is characterized by more complicated and more difficult language and by more complicated grammatical structures. Short forms and contractions are avoided in **formal** speech and writing. *See* INFORMAL.

formula refers to set phrases that are used in certain conventions, as in 'How do you do?', 'Yours faithfully', 'Yours sincerely', 'Kind regards', 'See you later', 'Nice to see you!' and 'Many happy returns'.

form word *see* **function word**.

-free is a suffix used to form adjectives indicating 'absence of, freedom from', as in 'carefree', 'trouble-free', 'anxiety-free', 'tax-free', 'duty-free', 'additive-free', 'lead-free'.

-friendly is a modern suffix formed on analogy with 'user-friendly' to mean 'helpful to, supporting', as in 'child-friendly', 'environment-friendly' and 'ozone-friendly'.

frequentative refers to a verb which expresses frequent repetition of an action. In English the verb endings *-le* and *-el* sometimes indicate the **frequentative** form, as in 'waddle' from 'wade', 'sparkle' from 'spark', 'crackle' from 'crack' and 'dazzle' from 'daze'. The ending *-er* can also indicate the **frequentative** form, as in 'stutter', 'spatter' and 'batter'.

-ful is a suffix indicating 'the amount that fills something', as in 'bucketful', 'basinful', 'handful', 'spoonful', 'bagful' and 'pocketful'. It can also mean 'full of', as in 'beautiful', 'truthful' and 'scornful'. It can also mean 'having the qualities of', as in 'masterful' and 'apt to, able to', as in 'forgetful', 'mournful' and 'useful'.

full stop is a punctuation mark consisting of a small dot. Its principal use is to end a sentence that is not a question or an exclamation, as in 'They spent the money.', 'She is studying hard.', 'He has been declared redundant and is very upset.' and 'Because she is shy, she rarely goes to parties.'

The **full stop** is also used in decimal fractions, as in '4.5 metres', '6.3 miles' and '12.2 litres'. It can also be used in dates, as in '22.2.94', and in times, as in '3.15 tomorrow afternoon'.

In modern usage the tendency is to omit **full stops** from
abbreviations. This is most true of abbreviations involving initial capital letters as in TUC, BBC, EEC and USA.
In such cases full stops should definitely not be used if
one or some of the initial letters do not belong to a full
word. Thus, television is abbreviated to TV and educationally subnormal to ESN.

There are usually no full stops in abbreviations involving the first and letters of a word (contractions) Dr, Mr,
Rd, St, but this is a matter of taste.

Abbreviations involving the first few letters of a word,
as in 'Prof' (Professor) are the most likely to have full
stops, as in 'Feb.' (February), but again this is now a matter of taste.

For the use of the **full stop** in direct speech *see* DIRECT
SPEECH. The **full stop** can also be called **point** or **period**.

function word is a word that has very little meaning but is
primarily of grammatical significance and merely performs a 'function' in a sentence. **Function words** include
determiners, and prepositions, such as in, on and up.
Words which are not **function words** are sometimes
known as 'content words'.

Function word is also known as **form word** or **structure word**.

future tense describes actions or states that will occur at
some future time. It is marked by 'will' and 'shall'. Traditionally 'shall' was used with subjects in the first person,
as in 'I shall see you tomorrow' and 'We shall go there
next week', and 'will' was used with subjects in the second and third person, as in 'You will find out next week',

'He will recognize her when he sees her' and 'They wi be on the next train'. Formerly 'will' was used with th first person and 'shall' with the second and third person t indicate emphasis or insistence, as in 'I *will* go on m own' and 'We *will* be able to afford it'; 'You *shall* pa what you owe' and 'The children *shall* get a holiday'. I modern usage 'shall' is usually used only for emphasis c insistence, whether with the first, second or third perso except in formal contexts. Otherwise 'will' is used, as i 'I will go tomorrow', 'We will have to see', 'You will b surprised', and 'They will be on their way by now'.

The **future tense** can also be marked by 'be about to plus the infinitive of the relevant verb or 'be going to plus the infinitive of the relevant verb. Examples includ 'We are about to leave for work', 'They are about to go o holiday', 'She is going to be late' and 'They are going t demolish the building'.

future perfect tense is formed by 'will' or 'shall' togethe with the 'perfect tense', as in 'They will have been mar ried ten years next week', 'You will have finished worl by this time tomorrow' and 'By the time Jane arrives her she will have been travelling non-stop for forty-eigh hours'.

G

gate is a modern suffix which is added to a noun to indicate something scandalous. Most of the words so formed are short-lived and forgotten about almost as soon as they are invented. In modern usage they are frequently used to apply to sexual scandals, but originally **-gate** was restricted to some form of political scandal. The suffix is derived from **Watergate**, and refers to a political scandal in the United States during President Richard Nixon's re-election campaign in 1972, when Republican agents were caught breaking into the headquarters of the Democratic Party in Washington, which were in a building called the Watergate Building. The uncovering of the attempts to cover up the break-in led to Richard Nixon's resignation.

gemination refers to the doubling of consonants before a suffix. *See* DOUBLING OF CONSONANTS.

gender in the English language usually refers to the natural distinctions of sex (or absence of sex) that exist, and nouns are classified according to these distinctions—masculine, feminine and neuter. Thus, 'man', 'boy', 'king', 'prince', 'emperor', 'duke', 'heir', 'son', 'brother', 'father', 'nephew', 'husband', 'bridegroom', 'widower', 'hero', 'cock', 'drake', 'fox' and 'lion' are masculine nouns. Similarly, 'girl', 'woman', 'queen', 'princess', 'empress', 'duchess', 'heiress', 'daughter', 'sister' 'mother', 'niece', 'wife', 'bride', 'widow', 'heroine' 'hen', 'duck', 'vixen' and 'lioness' are feminine nouns. Similarly, 'table', 'chair', 'desk', 'carpet', 'window' 'lamp', 'car', 'shop', 'dress', 'tie', 'newspaper', 'book' 'building' and 'town' are all neuter.

Some nouns in English can refer either to a man or woman, unless the sex is indicated in the context. Such neutral nouns are sometimes said to have **dual gender** Examples include 'author', 'singer', 'poet', 'sculptor' 'proprietor', 'teacher', 'parent', 'cousin', 'adult' and 'child'. Some words in this category were formerly automatically assumed to be masculine and several of them had feminine forms, such as 'authoress', 'poetess' 'sculptress' and 'proprietrix'. In modern times this was felt to be sexist and many of these feminine forms are now rarely used, for example, 'authoress' and 'poetess'. However some, such as actress and waitress, are still in common use. *See* -ESS.

In many languages **grammatical gender** plays a major part. In French, for example, all nouns are divided into masculine and feminine, and there is no neuter classification. Masculine nouns are preceded by *le* (definite article). Thus 'ceiling' is masculine (*le plafond*), 'hat' is masculine (*le chapeau*) and 'book' is masculine (*le livre*). Feminine nouns are preceded by *la* (definite article). Thus 'door' is feminine (*la porte*), 'dress' is feminine (*la robe*) and 'window' is feminine (*la fenêtre*).

In German there are three grammatical genders—masculine, feminine and neuter. Masculine nouns are preceded by *der* (definite article) as *der Stuhl* (the chair); feminine nouns are preceded by *die* (definite article) as *die Brücke* (the bridge); neuter nouns are preceded by *das*, as *das Brot* (bread).

Grammatical gender in English is not relevant except in the third personal singular pronouns, as 'he/him/his/ himself', 'she/her/hers/herself' and 'it/it/its/itself'. Traditionally 'he', etc, was considered an acceptable pronoun not just for nouns of the masculine gender, but also for those of neutral or dual gender as well. Thus 'Every student must check that he has registered for the exam' was considered acceptable, as was 'Each passenger must be responsible for his own luggage'. Nowadays such sentences are considered sexist. In order to avoid this, some people use the 'he/she', 'his/her', etc, convention, as in 'Every employee must supply his/her own transport' and 'Each candidate must hand in his/her application form now'. People who feel this is clumsy sometimes prefer to be ungrammatical and use a plural pronoun, as in 'Every writer was told to collect their manuscripts in person' and 'Every pupil was told that they would have to be back in school by four o'clock'. It is sometimes possible to avoid being both sexist and ungrammatical by rephrasing such sentences in the plural, as in 'All pupils were told that they would have to be back in school by four o'clock'.

enitive case indicates possession or ownership. It is usually marked by *s* and an apostrophe. Many spelling errors centre on the position of the *s* in relation to the apostrophe.

Nouns in the **genitive case** are usually formed by add-

ing 's to the singular noun, as in 'the girl's mother', an
Peter's car'; by adding an apostrophe to plural nouns tha
end in s, as in 'all the teachers' cars' and 'the doctors' sur
geries'; by adding 's to irregular plural nouns that do no
end in s, as in 'women's shoes'.

In the genitive form of a name or singular noun which
ends in s, x or z, the apostrophe may or may not be fol
lowed by s. In words of one syllable the final s is usually
added, as in 'James's house', 'the fox's lair', 'Roz'
dress'.

The final s is most frequently omitted in names, particu
larly in names of three or more syllables, as in 'Euripides
plays'.

In many cases the presence or absence of final s is
matter of convention.

Apostrophes are often omitted wrongly in modern us
age, particularly in the media and by advertisers, as ii
'womens hairdressers', 'childrens helpings'. In addition
apostrophes are frequently added erroneously (as in 'po
tato's for sale' and 'Beware of the dog's'). This is partly
because people are unsure about when and when not t
use them and partly because of a modern tendency t
punctuate as little as possible.

A group **genitive** occurs when more than one noun is in
volved, as in 'Gilbert and Sullivan's operas'. Note there i
only one apostrophe s.

The alternative genitive construction involves the use o
'of', as in 'the mother of the girl', 'the uncle of the littl
girl', 'the pages of the newspaper' and 'the leg of th
chair'. In general, proper nouns and animate beings ten

to take the apostrophe and *s* ending and inanimate objects tend to take the 'of' construction.

geo- is a prefix derived from Greek indicating 'earth', as in 'geography', 'geology', 'geomagnetic' and 'geophysics'.

geographical features should be written with initial capital letters. These include the common nouns that are part of the name of the feature, as in 'Niagara Falls', 'Atlantic Ocean', 'River Thames', 'Mount Everest' and 'Devil's Island'.

gerund refers to the *-ing* form of a verb when it functions as a noun. It is sometimes known as a **verbal noun**. It has the same form as the present participle but has a different function. For example, in the sentence 'He was jogging down the road', 'jogging' is the present participle in the verb phrase 'was jogging', but in the sentence 'Running is his idea of relaxation', 'running' is a gerund because it acts as a noun as the subject of the sentence. Similarly, in the sentence 'We were smoking when the teacher found us', 'smoking' is the present participle in the verb phrase 'were smoking', but in the sentence 'We were told that smoking is bad for our health', 'smoking' is a gerund since it acts as a noun as the subject of the clause.

get is sometimes used to form the passive voice instead of the verb 'to be'. The use of the verb 'to **get**' to form the passive, as in 'They get married tomorrow', 'Our team got beaten today' and 'We got swindled by the con man' is sometimes considered to be more informal than the use of 'be'. Often there is more action involved when the **get** construction is used than when 'be' is used, since **get** is a more dynamic verb, as in 'She was late leaving the pub

because she got involved in an argument' and in 'It was
her own fault that she got arrested by the police. She hit
one of the constables'.

Get is frequently overused. Such overuse should be
avoided, particularly in formal contexts. **Get** can often be
replaced by a synonym such as 'obtain', 'acquire', 'receive', 'get hold of', etc. Thus, 'If you are getting into
money difficulties you should get some financial advice.
Perhaps you could get a bank loan' could be rephrased as
'If you are in financial difficulty you should obtain some
financial help. Perhaps you could receive a bank loan'.

Got, the past tense of **get**, is often used unnecessarily, as
in 'She has got red hair and freckles' and 'We have got
enough food to last us the week'. In these sentences 'has'
and 'have' are sufficient on their own.

gliding vowel means the same as **diphthong**.

goal can be used to describe the recipient of the action of a
verb, the opposite of 'agent' or 'actor'. Thus, in the sentence 'The boy hit the girl', 'boy' is the 'agent' or 'actor'
and 'girl' is the **goal**. Similarly, in the sentence 'The dog
bit the postman', 'dog' is the 'agent' or 'actor' and 'postman' is the **goal**.

gobbledygook is used informally to refer to pretentious and
convoluted language of the type that is found in official
documents and reports. It is extremely difficult to understand and should be avoided and 'plain English' used instead.

govern is used of a verb or preposition in relation to a noun
or pronoun and indicates that the verb or preposition has a
noun or pronoun depending on it. Thus, in the phrase 'on

the table', 'on' is said to govern 'table'.

gradable is used of adjectives and adverbs and means that they can take degrees of comparison. Thus 'clean' is a **gradable** adjective since it has a comparative form (cleaner) and a superlative form (cleanest). 'Soon' is a **gradable** adverb since it has a comparative form (sooner) and a superlative form (soonest). Such words as 'supreme', which cannot normally have a comparative or superlative form, are called **non-gradable**.

gram is a suffix derived from Greek indicating 'writing' or 'drawing', as in 'telegram', 'electrocardiogram' and 'diagram'. It is also used in modern usage to indicate a 'greeting' or 'message', as in 'kissogram'.

graph is a suffix derived from Greek indicating 'written, recorded, represented', as in 'autograph', 'monograph', 'photograph'. It is also used to indicate 'an instrument that records', as in 'seismograph', 'tachograph' and 'cardiograph'.

group noun means the same as **collective noun**.

gynaec(o)- is a prefix derived from Greek indicating 'female, woman', as in 'gynaecology', 'gynaecium'.

H

habitual refers to the action of a verb that occurs regularly and repeatedly.. The **habitual present** is found in such sentences as 'He goes to bed at ten every night', 'She always walks to work' and 'The old man sleeps all day'. This is in contrast to the 'stative present', which indicates the action of the verb that occurs at all times, as in 'Cows chew the cud', 'Water becomes ice when it freezes', 'Children grow up' and 'We all die'. Examples of the **habitual past** tense include; 'They travelled by train to work all their lives', 'We worked twelve hours a day on that project' and 'She studied night and day for the exams'.

-hand is a suffix meaning 'worker', as in 'deckhand', 'farmhand' and 'cowhand'. It can also mean 'position', as in 'right-hand' and 'left-hand'.

haem(o)- is a prefix derived from Greek meaning 'blood', as in 'haemorrhage', 'haematology' and 'haematoma'.

haiku refers to a short Japanese poem in three unrhymed lines with an exact number of syllables per line, the syllable pattern being 5-7-5. The traditional subject matter is usually something to do with nature. A master of the form was the 17th-century Japanese poet Basho, and the following is one of his haiku:

The | white | chry|san|themum
Even | when | lif|ted | to | the | eye
Re|mains | im|macu|late.

half and **halve** are liable to be confused. **Half** is a noun and
halve is a verb. **Half** is followed by a singular noun when
it is referring to an amount, as in 'Half of the milk has
gone sour' and 'Half the money is hers'. It is followed by
a plural verb when it is referring to a number, as in 'Half
of the people are still undecided' and 'Half of the sweets
are for the younger children'. The plural of **half** is **halves**,
as in 'They cut the oranges in two and distributed the
halves to the members of the two teams'.

The plural noun **halves** is liable to be confused with the
verb **halve**. Examples of the noun **halves** include 'They
served halves of grapefruit for breakfast' and 'He split the
estate into halves and left it to his son and daughter'. Examples of the verb **halve** include 'halve the grapefruit for
breakfast' and 'He decided to halve his estate between his
son and daughter'.

hanged and **hung** are both past tense and past participles of
the verb 'to hang' but they are not interchangeable. **Hung**
is the more usual form, as in 'The children hung their out-
door clothes on pegs outside the classroom', 'They hung
the portrait of her father in the dining room', 'Dark clouds
of smoke hung over the city' and 'The boy has hung
around with the same crowd of friends for years'.
Hanged is restricted to the meaning 'suspended by the
neck until dead', as in 'They hanged him for the murder
of his wife in the 1920s', 'The murderer took his own life
before he could be hanged', 'They had to break the news

to the children that their father had hanged himself' and 'She hanged herself while the balance of her mind was disturbed'

hanging participle *see* **dangling participle**.

have is a verb which has several functions. A major use is its part in forming the 'perfect tense' and 'past perfect tense', or 'pluperfect tense', of other verb tenses. It does this in conjunction with the 'past participle' of the verb in question.

The perfect tense of a verb is formed by the present tense of the verb **have** and the past participle of the verb. Examples include 'We have acted wisely', 'They have beaten the opposition', 'The police have caught the thieves', 'The old man has died', 'The child has eaten all the food', 'The baby has fallen downstairs', 'They have grabbed all the bargains', 'You have hated him for years' and 'He has indicated that he is going to retire'. The past perfect or pluperfect is formed by the past tense of the verb **have** and the past participle of the verb in question, as in 'He had jumped over the fence', 'They had kicked in the door', 'The boy had led the other children to safety', 'His mother had made the cake', 'The headmaster had punished the pupils' and 'They had rushed into buying a new house'. Both perfect tenses and past perfect or pluperfect tenses are often contracted in speech or in informal written English, as in 'We've had enough for today', 'You've damaged the suitcase', 'You've missed the bus', 'He's lost his wallet', 'She's arrived too late', 'They'd left before the news came through', 'She'd married without telling her parents', 'He'd packed the goods himself' and

'You'd locked the door without realizing it'.

Have is often used in the phrase **have to** in the sense that something must be done. In the present tense **have to** can be used instead of 'must', as in 'You have to leave now', 'We have to clear this mess up', 'He has to get the next train' and 'The goods have to be sold today'. If the 'something that must be done' refers to the future the verb **will have to** is used', as in 'He will have to leave now to get there on time', 'The old man will have to go to hospital' and 'They'll have to move out of the house when her parents return'. If the 'something that must be done' refers to the past, **had to** is used, as in 'We had to take the injured man to hospital', 'They had to endure freezing conditions on the mountain', 'They'd to take a reduction in salary' and 'We'd to wait all day for the workman to appear'.

Have is also used in the sense of 'possess' or 'own', as in 'He has a swimming pool behind his house ', 'She has a huge wardrobe', 'We have enough food' and 'They have four cars'. In spoken or in informal English 'have got' is often used, as in 'They've got the largest house in the street', 'We've got problems now', 'They haven't got time'. This use should be avoided in formal English.

Have is also used to indicate suffering from an illness or disease, as in 'The child has measles', 'Her father has flu' and 'She has heart disease'. **Have** can also indicate that an activity is taking place, as in 'She's having a shower', 'We're having a party', 'She is having a baby' and 'They are having a dinner party'.

he is a personal pronoun and is used as the subject of a sentence or clause to refer to a man, boy, etc. It is thus said to be a 'masculine' personal pronoun. Since he refers to a third party and does not refer to the speaker or the person being addressed , it is a 'third-person pronoun'. Examples include 'James is quite nice but he can be boring', 'Bob has got a new job and he is very pleased' and 'He is rich but his parents are very poor'.

He traditionally was used not only to refer to nouns relating to the masculine sex but also to nouns that are now regarded as being neutral or of 'dual gender'. Such nouns include 'architect', 'artist', 'athlete', 'doctor', 'passenger', 'parent', 'pupil', 'singer', 'student'. Without further information from the context it is impossible to know to which sex such nouns are referring. In modern usage it is regarded as sexist to assume such words to be masculine by using **he** to refer to one of them unless the context indicates that the noun in question refers to a man or boy. Formerly it was considered acceptable to write or say 'Send a message to the architect who designed the building that he is to attend the meeting' whether or not the writer or speaker knew that the architect was a man. Similarly it was considered acceptable to write or say 'Please tell the doctor that he is to come straight away' whether or not the speaker or writer knew that the doctor was in fact a man. Nowadays this convention is considered sexist. In order to avoid sexism it is possible to use the convention 'he/ she', as in 'Every pupil was told that he/she was to be smartly dressed for the occasion', 'Each passenger was informed that he/she was to arrive ten minutes before the coach was due to leave' and 'Tell the doctor that he/she is required urgently'. However this convention is regarded by some people as being clumsy, particularly in spoken English or in informal written English. Some people prefer to be ungrammatical and use the plural personal pronoun 'they' instead of 'he/she' in certain situations, as in 'Every passenger was told that they had to arrive ten minutes before the coach was due to leave' and 'Every student was advised that they should apply for a college place by March'. In some cases it may be possible to rephrase sentences and avoid being either sexist or ungrammatical, as in 'All the passengers were told that they should arrive ten minutes before the coach was due to leave' and 'All students were advised that they should apply for a college place by March'.

headline is the name given to the title of a newspaper article. From the very nature of headlines they are short, partly because of shortage of space and partly to capture the attention of the would-be reader. In order to achieve this, the definite and indefinite articles and other minor words tend to be omitted, the future tense represented by a to-infinitive, as in 'Prescription charges to rise', and the present tenses used for past events. **Headline** language, particularly that of tabloid newspapers which has to be especially succinct and eye-catching, can have an effect on the general language. Thus expressions such as 'tug-of-love', which describes the state of a child whose custody is being bitterly fought over by both parents, is now quite common in the general language but started out as a headline term. Other expressions which are typical of the language of the headlines include 'killing spree', which describes someone who loses control and kills, usually by shooting, several people indiscriminately, as in 'Local gunman goes on killing spree'. Another one is 'have-a-go', which describes an attempt by a member of the public to try and catch a criminal, as in 'Pensioner in have-a-go with bank-raider'. The language and style of **headlines** is frequently known as **headlinese**.

heading refers to a word, phrase or sentence put at the top of a page, chapter, section, etc, of a book or other printed document. These are sometimes written with initial capital letters (except for articles or prepositions), as in 'Annual Report', 'Department Budget for the Year', 'The Year Ahead', 'What Went Wrong', 'Company Plans', 'Trading Outlook Overseas', but this is a matter of taste or of house style . Some people prefer to use lower-case letters except for the first word, as in 'Sales targets for the year', 'A review of export markets', and 'The way forward'. Headings can be underlined or placed in italic type or bold type to highlight them on the page.

headword refers to a word which is at the head of an entry in a dictionary or other reference book. It is also known as 'entry word' and is usually written in bold type so that it stands out on the page and is readily identifiable.

helping verb is another name for **auxiliary verb**.

hemi- is a prefix derived from Greek meaning 'half', as in 'hemisphere' and 'hemiplegia'.

hendiadys is a figure of speech in which two nouns joined by 'and' are used to express an idea that would normally be expressed by the use of an adjective and a noun, as in 'through storm and weather' instead of 'through stormy weather'.

he/she *see* **he**.

her is a personal pronoun. It is the third person singular, is feminine in gender and acts as the object in a sentence, as in 'We saw her yesterday', 'I don't know her', 'He hardly ever sees her', 'Please give this book to her', 'Our daughter sometimes plays with her' and 'We do not want her to come to the meeting'. *See* **he**; **she**.

hers is a personal pronoun. It is the third person singular, feminine in gender and is in the poassessive case. 'The car is not hers', 'I have forgotten my book but I don't want to borrow hers', 'This is my seat and that is hers', and 'These clothes are hers'. *See* **his**; **her** and **possessive**.

hetero- is a prefix derived from Greek meaning 'other, another, different', as in 'heterodox' and 'heterosexual'.

hexa- is a prefix derived from Greek meaning 'six', as in 'hexagram' and 'hexagon'.

hiatus refers to a break in pronunciation between two vowels that come together in different syllables, as in 'Goyaesque' and 'cooperate'.

him is the third person masculine personal pronoun when used as the object of a sentence or clause, as in 'She shot him', 'When the police caught the thief they arrested him' and 'His parents punished him after the boy stole the money'. Traditionally **him** was used to apply not only to masculine nouns, such as 'man' and 'boy', but also to nouns that are said to be 'of dual gender'. These include 'architect', 'artist', 'parent', 'passenger', 'pupil' and 'student'. Without further information from the context, it is not possible for the speaker or writer to know the sex of the person referred to by one of these words. Formerly it was acceptable to write or say 'The artist must bring an easel with him' and 'Each pupil must bring food with him'. In modern usage this convention is considered sexist and there is a modern convention that 'him/her' should be used instead to avoid sexism, as in 'The artist must bring an easel with him/her' and 'Each pupil must bring food with him/her'. This convention is felt by some people to be clumsy, particularly in spoken and in informal English, and some people prefer to be ungrammatical and use the plural personal pronoun 'them' instead, as in 'The artist must bring an easel with them' and 'Each pupil must bring food with them'. In some situations it is possible to avoid being either sexist or ungrammatical by rephrasing the sentence, as in 'All artists must bring easels with them' and 'All pupils must bring food with them. *See* **he**.

him/her *see* **him**.

his is the third personal masculine pronoun when used to indicate possession, as in 'He has hurt his leg', 'The boy has taken his books home' and 'Where has your father left his tools?' Traditionally **his** was used to refer not only to masculine nouns, such as 'man', 'boy', etc, but to what are known as nouns 'of dual gender'. These include 'architect', 'artist', 'parent', 'passenger', 'pupil' and 'student'. Without further information from the context it is not possible for the speaker or the writer to know the sex of the person referred to by one of these words. Formerly it was considered acceptable to use **his** in such situations, as in 'Every pupil has to supply his own sports equipment' and 'Every passenger is responsible for his own luggage'. In modern usage this is now considered sexist and there is a modern convention that 'his/her' should be used instead to avoid sexism, as in 'Every pupil has to supply his/her own sports equipment' and 'Every passenger is responsible for his/her own luggage'. This convention is felt by some people to be clumsy, particularly when used in spoken or informal written English. Some people prefer to be ungrammatical and use the plural personal pronoun 'their', as in 'Every pupil must supply their own sports equipment' and 'Every passenger is to be responsible for their own luggage'. In some situations it is possible to avoid being sexist, clumsy and ungrammatical by rephrasing the sentence, as in 'All pupils must supply their own sports equipment' and 'All passengers are to be responsible for their own luggage.

his/her *see* **his**

holidays, in the sense of public holidays or festivals, should be written with an initial capital letter, as in 'Christmas Day', 'Easter Sunday', 'New Year' and 'Independence Day'.

holo- is a prefix meaning 'complete, whole', as in 'holistic'.

homo- is a prefix derived from Greek meaning 'same', as in 'homogenous', 'homonym', 'homograph', 'homophone' and 'homosexual'.

homograph refers to a word that is spelt the same as another word but has a different meaning and pronunciation. **Homographs** include:

bow, pronounced to rhyme with 'how', a verb meaning 'to bend the head or body as a sign of respect or in greeting, etc', as in 'The visitors bowed to the emperor' and

'The mourners bowed their heads as the coffin was lowered into the grave'.

bow, pronounced to rhyme with 'low', a noun meaning 'a looped knot, a ribbon tied in this way', as in 'She tied her hair in a bow' and 'She wears blue bows in her hair'.

lead, pronounced 'leed', a verb meaning 'to show the way', as in 'The guide will lead you down the mountain'.

lead, pronounced 'led', a noun meaning 'a type of greyish metal', as in 'They are going to remove any water pipes made from lead'.

row, pronounced to rhyme with 'low', a noun meaning 'a number of people or things arranged in a line', as in 'The princess sat in the front row'.

row, pronounced to rhyme with 'how', a noun meaning 'a quarrel, a disagreement', as in 'He has had a row with his neighbour over repairs to the garden wall'.

slough, pronounced to rhyme with 'rough', a verb meaning 'to cast off', as in 'The snake had sloughed off its old skin'.

slough, pronounced to rhyme with 'how', a noun meaning 'a swamp', as in 'Get bogged down in a slough' and 'in the Slough of Despond'.

sow, pronounced to rhyme with 'low', a verb meaning 'to scatter seeds in the earth', as in 'In the spring the gardener sowed some flower seeds in the front garden'.

sow, pronounced to rhyme with 'how', a noun meaning 'a female pig', as in 'The sow is in the pigsty with her piglets'.

homonym refers to a word that has the same spelling and the same pronunciation as another word but has a different meaning from it. Examples include:

bill, a noun meaning 'a written statement of money owed', as in 'You must pay the bill for the conversion work immediately', or 'a written or printed advertisement', as in 'We were asked to deliver handbills advertising the play'.

bill, a noun meaning 'a bird's beak', as in 'The seagull has injured its bill'.

fair, an adjective meaning 'attractive', as in 'fair young women'; 'light in colour', as in 'She has fair hair'; 'fine, not raining', as in 'I hope it keeps fair'; 'just, free from prejudice', as in 'We felt that the referee came to a fair decision'.

fair, a noun meaning 'a market held regularly in the same place, often with stalls, entertainments and rides' (now often simply applying to an event with entertainments and rides without the market), as in 'He won a coconut at the fair'; 'a trade exhibition', as in 'the Frankfurt Book Fair'.

pulse, a noun meaning 'the throbbing caused by the contractions of the heart', as in 'The patient has a weak pulse'.

pulse, a noun meaning 'the edible seeds of any of various crops of the pea family, as lentils, peas and beans', as in 'Vegetarians eat a lot of food made with pulses'.

row, a verb meaning 'to propel a boat by means of oars', as in 'He plans to row across the Atlantic single-handed'.

row, a noun meaning 'a number of people or things arranged in a line', as in 'We tried to get into the front row to watch the procession' and 'The gardener has planted rows of cabbages'.

homonym is sometimes used to describe words that are more correctly classified as **homographs** or **homophones**. *See* **homograph**; **homophone**.

homophone refers to a word that is pronounced in the same way as another but is spelt in a different way and has a different meaning. **Homophones** include:

aisle, a noun meaning 'a passage between rows of seats in a church, theatre, cinema etc', as in 'The bride walked down the aisle on her father's arm'.

isle, a noun meaning 'an island', as in 'the Isle of Wight'.

alter, a verb meaning 'to change', as in 'They have had to alter their plans'.

altar, a noun meaning 'in the Christian church, the table on which the bread and wine are consecrated for Communion and which serves as the centre of worship', as in 'The priest moved to the altar, from where he dispensed Communion', 'There is a holy painting above the altar' or 'a raised structure on which sacrifices are made or incense burned in worship', as in 'The Druids made human sacrifices on the altar of their gods'.

ail, a verb meaning 'to be ill', as in 'The old woman is ailing'; 'to be the matter, to be wrong', as in 'What ails you?'

ale, a noun meaning 'a kind of beer', as in 'a pint of foaming ale'.

blew, a verb, the past tense of the verb 'blow', as in 'They blew the trumpets loudly'.

blue, a noun and adjective meaning 'a colour of the shade of a clear sky', as in 'She wore a blue dress'.

boar, a noun meaning 'a male pig', as in 'a dish made

with wild boar'.

bore, a verb meaning 'to make tired and uninterested', as in 'The audience was obviously bored by the rather academic lecture'.

bore, a verb, the past tense of the verb 'bear', as in 'They bore their troubles lightly'.

cereal, a noun meaning 'a plant yielding grain suitable for food', as in 'countries which grow cereal crops' and 'a prepared food made with grain', as in 'We often have cereal for breakfast'.

serial, a noun meaning 'a story or television play which is published or appears in regular parts, as in 'the final instalment of the magazine serial which she was following'.

cite, a verb meaning 'to quote or mention by way of example or proof', as in 'The lawyer cited a previous case to try and get his client off'.

sight, a noun meaning 'the act of seeing', as in 'They recognized him at first sight'.

site, a noun meaning 'a location, place', as in 'They have found a site for the new factory'.

feat, a noun meaning 'a notable act or deed', as in 'The old man received an award for his courageous feat'.

feet, a noun, the plural form of 'foot', as in 'The child got her feet wet from wading in the puddle'.

none, a pronoun meaning 'not any', as in 'They are demanding money but we have none'.

nun, a noun meaning 'a woman who joins a religious order and takes vows of poverty, chastity and obedience', as in 'She gave up the world to become a nun'.

know, a verb meaning 'to have understanding or knowl-

edge of', as in 'He is the only one who knows the true
facts of the situation', and 'to be acquainted with', as in '
met her once but I don't really know her'.

no, an adjective meaning 'not any', as in 'We have n(
food left'.

rite, a noun meaning 'a ceremonial act or words,' as i)
'rites involving witchcraft'.

right, an adjective meaning 'correct', as in 'Very few
people gave the right answer to the question'.

write, a verb meaning 'to form readable characters', as i)
'he writes regularly for the newspapers'.

stare, a verb and noun meaning 'to look fixedly' and '.
fixed gaze', as in 'She stared at him in disbelief when h(
told her the news' and 'He has the stare of a basilisk'.

stair, a noun meaning 'a series of flights of stairs', as i)
'The old lady is too feeble to climb the stairs to her bed
room'.

-hood is a suffix meaning 'state, condition', as in 'baby
hood', 'childhood', 'manhood', 'priesthood', 'woman
hood' and 'widowhood'.

hydro- is a prefix derived from Greek meaning 'water, as i)
'hydro-electric' and 'hydrophobia'. It also means 'hydro
gen', as in 'hydrochloride'.

hyper- is a prefix derived from Greek meaning 'over
above', as in 'hyperactive', 'hypercritical'
'hyperinflation' and 'hypersensitive'.

hypo- is a prefix derived from Greek meaning 'under', as i)
'hypothermia', 'hypodermic'.

hyphen refers to a small stroke used to join two words to
gether or to indicate that a word has been broken at th(

end of a line because of lack of space. It is used in a variety of situations.

The **hyphen** is used as the prefixed element in a proper noun, as in 'pre-Christian', 'post-Renaissance', 'anti-British', 'anti-Semitic', 'pro-French' and 'pro-Marxism'. It is also used before dates or numbers, as in 'pre-1914', 'pre-1066', 'post-1920', 'post-1745'. It is also used before abbreviations, as in 'pro-BBC', 'anti-EEC' and 'anti-TUC'.

The **hyphen** is used for clarification. Some words are ambiguous without the presence of a hyphen. For example, 're-cover', as in 're-cover a chair', is spelt with a hyphen to differentiate it from 'recover', as in 'The accident victim is likely to recover'. Similarly, it is used in 're-form', meaning 'to form again', as in 'They have decided to re-form the society which closed last year', to differentiate the word from 'reform', meaning 'to improve, to become better behaved', as in 'He was wild as a young man but he has reformed now'. Similarly 're-count' in the sense of 'count again' , as in 're-count the number of votes cast', is spelt with a hyphen to differentiate it from 'recount' in the sense of 'tell', as in 'recount what happened on the night of the accident'.

The **hyphen** was formerly used to separate a prefix from the main element of a word if the main element begins with a vowel, as in 'pre-eminent', but there is a growing tendency in modern usage to omit the **hyphen** in such cases. At the moment both 'pre-eminent' and 'preeminent' are found. However, if the omission of the **hyphen** results in double *i*, the **hyphen** is usually retained, as in 'anti-inflationary' and 'semi-insulated'.

The **hyphen** was formerly used in words formed with the prefix *non-*, as in 'non-functional', 'non-political', 'non-flammable' and 'non-pollutant'. However there is a growing tendency to omit the hyphen in such cases, as in 'nonfunctional' and 'nonpollutant'. At the moment both forms of such words are common.

The **hyphen** is usually used with 'ex-' in the sense of 'former', as in 'ex-wife' and 'ex-president'.

The **hyphen** is usually used when 'self-' is prefixed to words, as in 'self-styled', 'a self-starter' and 'self-evident'.

Use or non-use of the **hyphen** is often a matter of choice, house style or frequency of usage, as in 'drawing-room' or 'drawing room'. and 'dining-room' or 'dining room'. There is a modern tendency to punctuate less frequently than was formerly the case and so in modern usage use of the **hyphen** in such expressions is less frequent. The length of compounds often affects the inclusion or omission of the hyphen. Compounds of two short elements that are well-established words tend not to be hyphenated, as in 'bedroom' and 'toothbrush'. Compound words with longer elements are more likely to be hyphenated, as in 'engine-driver' and 'carpet-layer'.

Some fixed compounds of two or three or more words are always hyphenated, as in 'son-in-law', 'good-for-nothing' and 'devil-may-care'

Some compounds formed from phrasal verbs are sometimes hyphenated and sometimes not. Thus both 'take-over' and 'takeover' are common, and 'run-down' and 'rundown' are both common. Again the use of the hyphen is a matter of choice. However some words formed from phrasal verbs are usually spelt without a hyphen, as in 'breakthrough'.

Compound adjectives consisting of two elements, the second of which ends in *-ed*, are usually hyphenated, as in 'heavy-hearted', 'fair-haired', 'fair-minded' and 'long-legged'.

Compound adjectives when they are used before nouns are usually hyphenated, as in 'gas-fired central heating', 'oil-based paints', 'solar-heated buildings' and 'choco-late-coated biscuits'.

Compounds containing some adverbs are usually hyphenated, sometimes to avoid ambiguity, as in 'his best-known opera', a 'well-known singer', 'an ill-considered venture' and 'a half-planned scheme'.

Generally adjectives and participles preceded by an adverb are not hyphenated if the adverb ends in *-ly*, as in 'a highly talented singer', 'neatly pressed clothes' and 'beautifully dressed young women'.

In the case of two or more compound hyphenated adjectives with the same second element qualifying the same noun, the common element need not be repeated but the **hyphen** should be, as in 'two- and three-bedroom houses' and 'long- and short-haired dogs'.

The **hyphen** is used in compound numerals from 21 to 99 when they are written in full, as in 'thirty-five gallons', 'forty-four years', 'sixty-seven miles' and 'two hundred and forty-five miles'. Compound numbers such as 'three hundred' and 'two thousand' are not hyphenated.

Hyphens are used in fractions, as in 'three-quarters', 'two-thirds', and 'seven-eighths'.

Hyphens are also used in such number phrases as 'a seventeenth-century play', 'a sixteenth-century church', 'a five-gallon pail', 'a five-year contract' and a 'third-year student'.

The other use of **hyphens** is to break words at the end of lines. Formerly people were more careful about when they broke words. Previously, words were broken up according to etymological principles but there is a growing tendency to break words according to how they are pronounced. Some dictionaries or spelling dictionaries give help with the division and hyphenation of individual words. General points are that one-syllable words should not be divided and words should not be broken after the first letter of a word or before the last letter. Care should be taken not to break up words, for example by forming elements that are words in their own right, in such a way as to mislead the reader. Thus divisions such as 'the-rapist' and 'mans-laughter' should be avoided.

hybrid refers to a word that is formed from words or elements derived from different languages, such as 'television'.

hyperbole is a figure of speech consisting of exaggeration or over-statement, used for emphasis, as in 'I could eat a horse' and in 'I am boiling in this heat'.

I

and **me** are liable to be confused. They are both parts of the first person singular pronoun, but **I** acts as the subject of a sentence and **me** as the object. People often assume wrongly that **me** is less 'polite' than '**I**'. This is probably because they have been taught that in answer to such questions as 'Who is there?' the grammatically correct reply is 'It is I'. In fact, except in formal contexts, 'It is me' is frequently found in modern usage, especially in spoken contexts. Confusion arises as to whether to use **I** or **me** after 'between'. Since 'between' is followed by an object, **me** is the correct form. Thus it is correct to say 'Just between you and me, I think he is dishonest'. On the other hand, **me**, being an object, should not be used in such sentences as 'You and I have both been invited', 'May Jane and I play?' and 'The children and I are going to join you'. **Me** should, however, be used in such sentences as 'The cake was made by Mary and me', 'They were sitting in front of my son and me at the cinema' and 'My brother and father played against my mother and me', since in all these cases it is the object form of the first person singular that is required.

ian is a suffix either indicating 'a profession, job or pastime', as in 'comedian', 'musician', 'optician', 'physician', or indicating 'proper names', as in 'Elizabethan' 'Dickensian', 'Orwellian' and 'Shakesperian'.

-iana is a suffix form of -ana, indicating 'memorabilia o collections relating to people or places of note', as ir 'Victoriana' and 'Churchilliana'.

-ible *see* **adjectives**.

-ics is a suffix indicating 'science' or 'study', as in 'acoustics', 'electronics', 'genetics', 'obstetrics', 'politics' and 'physics'.

ideogram refers to a written character that symbolizes a word or phrase without indicating the pronunciation, such as £, &, +.

idiolect refers to the speech habits, knowledge and command of language of an individual. This can vary considerably from person to person. For example, one person might have a much more formal **idiolect** than another.

idiom refers to an expression whose meaning cannot be easily deduced from the individual meanings of the words it contains. Thus, in the expression 'know the ropes' one can know what 'know' means and know what 'ropes' means without being able to deduce the meaning of 'know the ropes'. In fact, 'know the ropes' is a nautical idiom. If a sailor was being taught the basics of seamanship in the days of sailing ships, he would have to be taught the mechanics of ropes which were an important part of sailing in those days. Hence, 'know the ropes' has come to mean 'to understand the procedures and details involved in something', as in 'When he first started the job the trainee mechanic felt really awkward and useless, but he when he knew the ropes he felt more confident and happier'.

Similarly, one can easily understand the meanings of the various individual words in the expression 'out on a limb', but it is not at all obvious that it means idiomatically 'in a risky and often lonely position', this being a reference to someone being stuck in an isolated and precarious position on the branch of a tree. This idiom is found in sentences such as 'The young designer has gone out on a limb and produced clothes that his boss says are too experimental for the mass market'. Literally it refers to a person or animal that has crawled so far out on a branch of a tree that he/she is in danger of falling or of not being able to crawl back to the main tree.

Similarly, in the expression 'throw someone to the lions' one can easily understand the meanings of the various individual words without realizing that the expression means 'deliberately to put someone in a difficult or dangerous position', as in 'All the teachers were responsible for the change in policy with regard to school uniform but they threw the deputy head to the lions when they asked him to address a parents' meeting on the subject'. In order to appreciate the meaning of the idiom fully, the reader or listener has to understand that the idiom refers to a supposed form of entertainment in ancient Rome in which prisoners were thrown to hungry wild animals to be attacked and killed (while spectators looked on enthusiastically).

Similarly, in the expression 'throw in the towel' one can easily understand the meanings of the various individual words without realizing that the phrase means 'to give in, to admit defeat', as in 'She tried to stand up to the bullies

in her school but finally she threw in the towel and aske
her parents to send her to another school'. This idiom
comes from the world of boxing in which 'throwing in th
towel' indicates a method of conceding defeat.

Similarly, understanding the individual words of the ex
pression 'sell someone down the river' will not help on
to understand that it means 'to betray or be disloyal t
someone', as in 'The bank robber who was caught by th
police refused to sell his associates down the river'. Th
origin here is slightly more obscure in that it refers his
torically to slave owners in the Mississippi states of th
United States, who sold their slaves to buyers dowr
stream in Louisiana where living and working condition
were much harder.

Such idioms as 'sell someone down the river' ar
known as 'opaque idioms' since there is no resemblanc
between the meaning of the individual words of the idior
and the idiom itself. Idioms such as 'keep a straight face
are known as 'transparent idioms' since, although the
are not to be interpreted literally, it is reasonably obviou
what they mean.

i.e. is the abbreviation of the Latin phrase *id est* and is use
before explanations or amplifications of what has jus
been mentioned, as in 'He was a mercenary in the war, i.e
he fought for money' and 'She is agoraphobic, i.e. she i
afraid of open spaces' and 'He is a bibliophile, i.e. h
loves books'. It is usually spelt with a full stop after eac
of the letters.

if is a conjunction which is often used to introduce a subor
dinate adverbial clause of condition, as in 'If he is talkin

of leaving he must be unhappy', 'If you tease the dog it
will bite you', 'If he had realized that the weather was going to be so bad he would not have gone on the expedi-
tion', 'If I had been in charge I would have sacked him'
and 'If it were a better organized firm things like that
would not happen'.

If can also introduce a 'nominal' or 'noun clause', as in
'He asked if we objected' and 'She inquired if we wanted
to go'.

ify is a suffix indicating 'making or becoming', as in
'beautify', 'clarify', 'dignify', 'purify', 'satisfy' and
'simplify'.

imperative mood is the verb mood that expresses commands. The verbs in the following sentences are in the
imperative mood. 'Go away!', 'Run faster!', 'Answer
me!', 'Sit down!', 'Please get out of here!'. All of these
expressions with verbs in the **imperative mood** sound
rather imperious or dictatorial and usually end with an exclamation mark, but this is not true of all expressions with
verbs in the **imperative mood**. For example, the following sentences all have verbs in the **imperative mood**:
'Have another helping of ice cream', 'Help yourself to
more wine', 'Just follow the yellow arrows to the X-ray
department', and 'Turn right at the roundabout'. Sentences with verbs in the **imperative mood** are known as
imperative sentences.

imperfect indicates a tense that denotes an action in
progress but not complete. The term derives from the
classification in Latin grammar and was traditionally applied to the 'past imperfect', as in 'They were standing

there'. The **imperfect** has now been largely supersede
by the 'progressive/continuous tense', which is marke
by the use of 'be' plus 'present participle'. Continuo
tenses are used when talking about temporary situatio
at a particular point in time, as in 'They were waiting f
the bus'.

impersonal refers to a verb which is used with a form
subject, usually 'it', as in 'It is raining' and 'They say
will snow tomorrow'.

indefinite article: **a** and **an** are the forms of the indefini
article. The form **a** is used before words that begin with
consonant sound, as 'a box', 'a garden', 'a road', 'a wal
The form **an** is used before words that begin with a vow
sound, as 'an apple', 'an easel', 'an ostrich', 'an uncle
Note that it is the sound of the initial letter that matte
and not the spelling. Thus **a** is used before words begin
ning with a *u* when they are pronounced with a *y* sound
though it were a consonant, as 'a unit', 'a usual occu
rence'. Similarly, **an** is used, for example, before word
beginning with the letter *h* where this is not pronounce
as in 'an heir', 'an hour', 'an honest man'.

Formerly it was quite common to use **an** before word
that begin with an *h* sound and also begin with an ur
stressed syllable, as in 'an hotel (ho-tel)', 'an histori
(his-tor-ik) occasion', 'an hereditary (her-ed-it-ary) dis
ease'. It is now more usual nowadays to use **a** in suc
cases and ignore the question of the unstressed syllable.

indefinite pronouns refer to people or things without bein
specific as to exactly who or what they are. They includ
'everyone', 'everybody', 'everything', 'anyone', 'any

body', 'anything', 'somebody', 'someone', 'something' and 'nobody', 'no one', 'nothing', as in 'Everyone is to make a contribution', 'Anyone can enter', 'Something will turn up' and 'Nobody cares'.

independent clause refers to a clause which can stand alone and make sense without being dependent on another clause, as in 'The children are safe'. Main clauses are **independent clauses**. Thus in the sentence 'She is tired and she wants to go home', there are two **independent clauses** joined by 'and'. In the sentence 'She will be able to rest when she gets home', 'She will be able to rest' is an **independent clause** and 'when she gets home' is a 'dependent clause'. In the sentence 'Because she is intelligent she thinks for herself', 'she thinks for herself' is an **independent clause** and 'because she is intelligent' is a 'dependent clause'.

indicative mood refers to the mood of a verb which denotes making a statement. The following sentences have verbs in the **indicative mood**: 'We go on holiday tomorrow', 'He was waiting for her husband', 'They have lost the match' and 'She will arrive this afternoon'. The **indicative mood** is sometimes known as the 'declarative mood'. The other moods are IMPERATIVE MOOD and SUBJUNCTIVE MOOD.

indirect object refers to an object which can be preceded by 'to' or 'for'. The **indirect object** usually refers to the person who benefits from an action or receives something as the result of it. In the sentence 'Her father gave the boy food', 'boy' is the **indirect object** and 'food' is the 'direct object'. The sentence could be rephrased as 'Her father

gave food to the boy'. In the sentence 'He bought hi
mother flowers', 'his mother' is the **indirect object** an
'flowers' is the 'direct object'. The sentence could hav
been rephrased as 'he bought flowers for his mother'. I
the sentence 'They offered him a reward', 'him' is the **in
direct object** and 'reward' is the 'direct object'. The sen
tence could be rephrased as 'They offered a reward t
him'.

indirect question refers to a question that is reported in in
direct speech, as in 'We asked them where they were go
ing', 'They inquired why we had come' and 'They looke
at us curiously and asked where we had come from'.

indirect speech is also known as **reported speech** and is
way of reporting what someone has said without using th
actual words used by the speaker. There is usually an in
troductory verb and a subordinate 'that' clause, as in 'H
said that he was going away', 'They announced that the
were leaving next day' and 'She declared that she ha
seen him there before'. In direct speech these sentence
would become 'He said, "I am going away"', 'They an
nounced, "We are leaving tomorrow"' and 'She declared
"I have seen him there before"'. When the change is mad
from 'direct speech' to **indirect speech**, the pronouns
adverbs of time and place and tenses are changed to ac
cord with the viewpoint of the person doing the reporting

infinitive refers to the 'base' form of a verb when used
without any indication of person, number or tense. There
are two forms of the **infinitive**. One is the 'to infinitive'
form, as in 'They wished to leave', 'I plan to go tomorrow', 'We aim to please' and 'They want to emigrate', 'To

know all is to forgive all', 'To err is human', 'Pull the lever to open', 'You should bring a book to read', 'The child has nothing to do', 'She is not very nice to know' and 'It is hard to believe that it happened'. The other form of the **infinitive** is called the **bare infinitive**. This form consists of the base form of the verb without 'to', as in 'We saw him fall', 'She watched him go', 'They noticed him enter', 'She heard him sigh', 'They let him go', 'I had better leave' and 'Need we return' and 'we dare not go back'. *See* SPLIT INFINITIVE.

inflect as applied to a word means to change form in order to indicate differences of tense, number, gender, case, etc. Nouns inflect for plural, as in 'ships', 'chairs', 'houses' and 'oxen'; nouns inflect for possessive, as in 'boys'', 'woman's', 'teachers'', and 'parents''; some adjectives inflect for the comparative form, as in 'brighter', 'clearer', 'shorter' and 'taller'; verbs inflect for the third person singular present tense, as in 'hears', 'joins', 'touches' and 'kicks'; verbs inflect for the present participle, as in 'hearing', 'joining', 'touching' and 'kicking'; verbs inflect for the past participle, as in 'heard', 'joined', 'touched' and 'kicked'.

inflection refers to the act of inflecting—*see* INFLECT. It also refers to an inflected form of a word or a suffix or other element used to inflect a word.

informal refers to a spoken or style of language that has a simpler grammatical structure and simpler vocabulary often involving vocabulary that is colloquial in nature or even slang.

infra- is a prefix derived from Latin indicating 'below, beneath', as in 'infrared' and 'infrastructure'.

-ing forms of verbs can be either PRESENT PARTICIPLES or GER
UNDS. Present participles are used in the formation of th
progressive or continuous tenses, as in 'We were lookin
at the pictures', 'Children were playing in the snow'
'They are waiting for the bus', 'Parents were showin
their anger', 'He has been sitting there for hours'. Prese
participles can also be used in non-finite clauses c
phrases, as in 'Walking along, she did not have a care i
the world', 'Lying there, he thought about his life', 'Sigl
ing, he left the room' and 'Smiling broadly he congrat
lated his friend'.

A large number of adjectives end in **-ing**. Many of thes
have the same form as the present participle of a transitiv
verb and are similar in meaning. Examples include 'a
amazing spectacle', 'a boring show', 'an interesting idea'
'a tiring day', 'an exhausting climb' and 'aching limbs'
Some **-ing** adjectives are related to intransitive verbs, a
'existing problems', 'increasing responsibilities', 'dwir
dling resources', 'an ageing work force' and 'prevailin
circumstances'. Some **-ing** adjectives are related to th
forms of verbs but have different meanings from th
verbs, as in 'becoming dress', 'an engaging personality'
'a dashing young man' and 'a retiring disposition'. Som
-ing adjectives are not related to verbs at all. These i
clude 'appetizing', 'enterprising', 'impending' and 'bal
ing'. Some **-ing** adjectives are used informally for empha
sis, as in 'a blithering idiot', 'a stinking cold' and 'a flam
ing cheek'.

Gerunds act as nouns and are sometimes known as 've

bal nouns'. Examples include 'Smoking is bad for one's health', 'Cycling is forbidden in the park' and 'Swimming is his favourite sport'.

intensifier refers to an adverb that affects the degree of intensity of another word. Intensifiers include 'thoroughly' in 'We were thoroughly shocked by the news', 'scarcely' in 'We scarcely recognized them' and 'totally' in 'She was totally amazed'.

inter- is a prefix of Latin origin indicating 'between', as in 'intercity', 'intercontinental' and 'interstate'.

interjections are kinds of 'exclamations'. Sometimes they are formed by actual words and sometimes they simply consist of sounds indicating emotional noises. Examples of **interjections** include 'Oh! I am quite shocked', 'Gosh! I'm surprised to hear that!', 'Phew! It's hot!', 'Ouch! That was my foot!', 'Tut-tut! He shouldn't have done that!' and 'Alas! She is dead.'

international Phonetic Alphabet is a system of written symbols designed to enable the speech sounds of any language to be consistently represented. Some of the symbols are the ordinary letters of the Roman alphabet but some have been specially invented. The alphabet was first published in 1889 and is commonly known a **IPA**.

interrogative adjective or **determiner** is an adjective or determiner that asks for information in relation to the nouns which they qualify, as in 'What dress did you choose in the end?', 'What kind of book are you looking for?', 'Which house do you like best?', 'Which pupil won the prize?', 'Whose bike was stolen?' and 'Whose dog is that?'

interrogative adverb is an adverb that asks a question, a
in 'When did they leave?', 'When does the meetin
start?', 'Where do they live?', 'Where was the stolen ca
found?', 'Where did you last see her?', 'Why was she cry
ing?', 'Why have they been asked to leave?', 'How is th
invalid?', 'How do you know that she has gone?' an
'Wherever did you find that?'

interrogative pronoun is a pronoun that asks a question, a
in 'Who asked you to do that?', 'Who broke the vase?'
'What did he say?, 'What happened next?', 'Whose ar
those books?', 'Whose is that old car?', 'To whom wa
that remark addressed?' and 'To whom did you addres
the package?'

interrogative sentence refers to a sentence that asks
question, as in 'Who is that?', 'Where is he?', 'Why hav
they appeared?', 'What did they take away?, 'Which d
you prefer?' and 'Whose baby is that?'. Sentences whic
take the form of an **interrogative question** do not alway
seek information. Sometimes they are exclamations, as i
'Did you ever see anything so beautiful?', 'Isn't sh
sweet?' and 'Aren't they lovely?'. Sentences which tak
the form of questions may really be commands or direc
tives, as in 'Could you turn down that radio?', 'Would yo
make less noise?' and 'Could you get her a chair?'. Sen
tences which take the form of questions may function a
statements, as in 'Isn't there always a reason?' an
'Haven't we all experienced disappointment?'. Some **in
terrogative sentences** are what are known as 'rhetorica
questions', which are asked purely for effect and requir
no answer, as in 'Do you think I am a fool?', 'What is th

point of life?' and 'What is the world coming to?'.

intra- is a prefix of Latin origin indicating 'within', as 'in-tramuscular', 'intra-uterine' and 'intravenous'.

intransitive verb refers to a verb that does not take a 'direct object', as in 'Snow fell yesterday', 'The children played in the sand', 'The path climbed steeply', 'Time will tell', 'The situation worsened', 'Things improved' and 'Prices increased'. Many verbs can be either transitive or intransitive, according to the context. Thus 'play' is **intransitive** in the sentence 'The children played in the sand' but 'transitive' in the sentence 'The boy plays the piano'. Similarly 'climb' is intransitive in the sentence 'The path climbs steeply' but transitive in the sentence 'The mountaineers climbed Everest'. Similarly 'tell' is **intransitive** in the sentence 'Time will tell' but 'transitive' in the sentence 'He will tell his life story'.

introductory it refers to the use of 'it' as the subject of a sentence in the absence of a meaningful subject. It is used particularly in sentences about time and the weather, as in 'It is midnight', 'It is dawn', 'It is five o'clock', 'It is twelve noon', 'It is raining', 'It was snowing', 'It was windy' and 'It was blowing a gale'.

intrusive r refers to the pronunciation of the *r* sound between two words or syllables where the first of these ends in a vowel sound and the second begins with a vowel sound and where there is no 'r' in the spelling. It appears in such phrases as 'law and order', which is frequently pronounced as 'lawr and order'.

invariable refers to a word whose form does not vary by inflection. Such words include 'sheep' and 'but'.

inversion refers to the reversal of the usual word order. It particularly refers to subjects and verbs. **Inversion** is used in questions, in some negative sentences, and for literary effect. In questions, an auxiliary verb is usually put in front of the subject and the rest of the verb group is put after the subject, as in 'Are you going to see her?' and 'Have they inspected the goods yet?'. The verb 'to do' is frequently used in **inversion**, as in 'Did he commit the crime?' and 'Do they still believe that?'. Examples of the use of **inversion** in negative sentences include 'Seldom have I witnessed such an act of selfishness', 'Never had she experienced such pain' and 'Rarely do we have time to admire the beauty of the countryside'. This use in negative sentences is rather formal.

  Inversion frequently involves adverbial phrases of place, as in 'Beyond the town stretched field after field', 'Above them soared the eagle' and 'Along the driveway grew multitudes of daffodils'.

  Inversion is also found in conditional clauses that are not introduced by conjunction, as in 'Had you arrived earlier you would have got a meal' and 'Had we some more money we could do more for the refugees'.

inverted commas, also called **quotation marks** and **quotes**, are used to enclose material that is part of reported speech. *See* REPORTED SPEECH. They can also be used instead of italic type in the titles of books, newspapers, magazines, plays, films, musical works, works of art, etc, as in 'The Times', 'Northanger Abbey' by Jane Austen, 'Two Gentlemen of Verona', 'The Silence of the Lambs' and 'The Mikado'. **Inverted commas** can also be

used to emphasize or draw attention to a particular word
or phrase, as in 'She wants to know how to spell "pic-
nicked"'. **Inverted** commas can either be single or double. If a word, phrase or passage is already contained
within quotes one should use the opposite style of **inverted commas** to the set already in use, as in 'She asked
how to pronounce "controversy"' or "She asked how to
pronounce 'controversy'".

irony indicates the use of a word or words to convey something that is completely different from the literal meaning,
as in 'I don't suppose you'd be interested to hear that your
house has been burgled', 'So you've crashed the car.
Thanks! That's a great help!'. *See* DRAMATIC IRONY.

irregular plurals refer to the plural form of nouns that do
not form their plural in the regular way. Most nouns in
English add -*s* to the singular form to form the plural
form, as in 'boy' to 'boys'. Some add -*es* to the singular
form to form the plural, as in 'church' to 'churches'.
Nouns ending in a consonant followed by -*y* have -*ies* as a
regular plural ending. Thus 'fairy' becomes 'fairies' and
'berry' becomes 'berries'. The foregoing are all examples
of 'regular plurals'.

Irregular plurals include words that are different in
form from the singular forms and do not simply add an
ending. These include 'men' from 'man', 'women' from
'woman' and 'mice' from 'mouse'. Some irregular plurals are formed by changing the vowel of the singular
forms, as in 'feet' from 'foot', 'geese' from 'goose' and
'teeth' from 'tooth'. Some irregular plural forms are
formed by adding -*en*, as 'oxen' from 'ox' and 'children'

from 'child'. Some nouns ending in *-f* form plurals in *-ves*, as in 'loaf' to 'loaves', 'half' to 'halves', 'wife' to 'wives' and 'wolf' to 'wolves', but some have alternative endings, as 'hoof' to either 'hoofs' or 'hooves', and some form regular plurals unchanged, as 'roof' to 'roofs'. Some irregular plural forms are the original foreign plural forms of words adopted into English, for example 'stimuli' from 'stimulus', 'phenomena' from 'phenomenon', 'criteria' from 'criterion', 'larvae' from 'larva'. In modern usage there is a growing tendency to anglicize the plural forms of foreign words. Many of these co-exist with the plural form, for example 'thesauruses' and 'thesauri', 'formulas' and 'formulae', 'gateaus' and 'gateaux' and 'indexes' and 'indices'. Sometimes the anglicized plural formed according to the regular English rules differs slightly in meaning from the irregular foreign plural. Thus 'indexes' usually applies to guides in books and 'indices' is usually used in mathematics. Some nouns have irregular plurals in that the plural form the singular form are the same. These include 'sheep', 'grouse' (the game bird) and 'salmon'. Some nouns have a regular plural and an irregular plural form .Thus 'brother' has the plural forms 'brothers' and 'brethren' although 'brethren' is now mainly used in a religious context and is archaic in general English.

irregular adjectives refer to adjectives that do not conform to the usual rules of forming the comparison and superlative. Many adjectives either add *-er* for the comparative and add *-est* for the superlative, as in 'taller', 'shorter' and 'tallest', 'shortest'. Some adjectives form their comparatives with 'more' and their superlatives with 'most', as in 'more beautiful', 'more practical' and 'most beautiful', 'most practical'. **Irregular adjectives** do not form their comparatives and superlatives in either of these ways. Irregular adjectives include:

positive	comparative	superlative
good	better	best
bad	worse	worst
little	less	least
many	more	most

irregular verbs are verbs that do not conform to the usual pattern of verbs in that some of their forms deviate from what one would expect if the pattern of regular verbs was being followed. There are four main forms of a regular verb—the INFINITIVE or 'base' form, as in 'hint', 'halt', 'hate' and 'haul'; the 'third-person singular' form as 'hints', 'halts', 'hates' and 'hauls'; the -ING form or 'present participle', as 'hinting', halting', 'hating' and 'hauling'; the -ed form or 'past tense' or 'past participle', as 'hinted', halted', 'hated' and 'hauled.

Irregular verbs deviate in some way from that pattern, in particular from the pattern of adding -ed to the past tense and past participle. They fall into several categories.

One category concerns those which have the same form in the past tense and past participle forms as the infinitive and do not end in -ed, like regular verbs. These include:

infinitive	past tense	past participle
bet	bet	bet
burst	burst	burst
cast	cast	cast

infinitive	past tense	past participle
cost	cost	cost
cut	cut	cut
hit	hit	hit
hurt	hurt	hurt
let	let	let
put	put	put
run	run	run
set	set	set
shed	shed	shed
shut	shut	shut
slit	slit	slit
split	split	split
spread	spread	spread

Some **irregular verbs** have two past tenses and two past participles which are the same, as in:

infinitive	past tense	past participle
burn	burned, burnt	burned, burnt,
dream	dreamed, dreamt	dreamed, dreamt,
dwell	dwelled, dwelt	dwelled, dwelt,
hang	hanged, hung,	hanged, hung
kneel	kneeled, knelt,	kneeled, knelt
lean	leaned, leant	learned, learnt
leap	leaped, leapt,	leaped, leapt
learn	learned, learnt	learned, learnt
light	lighted, lit	lighted, lit
smell	smelled, smelt	smelled, smelt
speed	speeded, sped	speeded, sped
spill	spilled, spilt	spilled, spilt
spoil	spoiled, spoilt	spoiled, spoilt

weave	weaved, woven	weaved, woven
wet	wetted, wet	wetted, wet,

Some **irregular verbs** have past tenses which do not end in *-ed* and have the same form as the past participle. These include:

infinitive	*past tense*	*past participle*
become	became	became
bend	bent	bent
bleed	bled	bled
breed	bred	bred
build	built	built
cling	clung	clung
come	came	came
dig	dug	dug
feel	felt	felt
fight	fought	fought
find	found	found
flee	fled	fled
fling	flung	flung
get	got	got
grind	ground	ground
hear	heard	heard
hold	held	held
keep	kept	kept
lay	laid	laid
lead	led	led
leave	left	left
lend	lent	lent
lose	lost	lost
make	made	made

infinitive	past tense	past participle
mean	meant	meant
meet	met	met
pay	paid	paid
rend	rent	rent
say	said	said
seek	sought	sought
sell	sold	sold
send	sent	sent
shine	shone	shone
shoe	shod	shod
sit	sat	sat
sleep	slept	slept
slide	slid	slid
sling	slung	slung
slink	slunk	slunk
spend	spent	spent
spin	spun	spun
stand	stood	stood
stick	stuck	stuck
sting	stung	stung
strike	struck	struck
string	strung	strung
sweep	swept	swept
swing	swung	swung
teach	taught	taught
tell	told	told
think	thought	thought
understand	understood	understood
weep	wept	wept

| win | won | won |
| wring | wrung | wrung |

Some **irregular verbs** have regular past tense forms but two possible past participles, one of which is regular. These include:

infinitive	*past tense*	*past participle*
mow	mowed	mowed, mown
prove	proved	proved, proven
sew	sewed	sewn, sewed
show	showed	showed, shown
sow	sowed	sowed, sown
swell	swelled	swelled, swollen

Some **irregular verbs** have past tenses and past participles that are different from each other and different from the infinitive. These include:

infinitive	*past tense*	*past participle*
arise	arose	arisen
awake	awoke	awoken
bear	bore	borne
begin	began	begun
bid	bade	bidden
bite	bit	bitten
blow	blew	blown
break	broke	broken
choose	chose	chosen
do	did	done
draw	drew	drawn
drink	drank	drunk
drive	drove	driven
eat	ate	eaten

infinitive	past tense	past participle
fall	fell	fallen
fly	flew	flown
forbear	forbore	forborne
forbid	forbade	forbidden
forgive	forgave	forgiven
forget	forgot	forgotten
forsake	forsook	forsaken
freeze	froze	frozen
forswear	forswore	forewarn
give	gave	given
go	went	gone
grow	grew	grown
hew	hewed	hewn
hide	hid	hidden
know	knew	known
lie	lay	lain
ride	rode	ridden
ring	rang	rung
saw	sawed	sawn
see	saw	seen
rise	rose	risen
shake	shook	shaken
shrink	shrank	shrunk
slay	slew	slain
speak	spoke	spoken
spring	sprang	sprung
steal	stole	stolen
stink	stank	stunk
strew	strewed	strewn

stride	strode	stridden
stride	strode	stridden
strive	strove	striven
swear	swore	sworn
swim	swam	swum
take	took	taken
tear	tore	torn
throw	threw	thrown
tread	trod	trodden
wake	woken	woke
wear	wore	worn
write	written	wrote

-ise and **-ize** are both verb endings. In British English there are many verbs which can be spelt ending in either **-ise** or **-ize**, as 'computerise/ize', 'economise/ize', 'finalist/ize', 'hospitalise/ize', 'modernise/ize', 'organise/ize', 'realise/ize', 'theorise/ize'. There are a few verbs which cannot be spelt **-ize**. These include 'advertise', 'advise', 'comprise', 'despise', 'exercise', 'revise', 'supervise' and 'televise'.

-ish is a suffix indicating 'somewhat', as in 'baldish', 'biggish', 'smallish', 'youngish', and 'nationality', as 'Spanish', 'Turkish' and 'Polish'.

-ism is a suffix indicating 'state, condition', as in 'alcoholism', 'fatalism', 'heroism' and 'plagiarism', or indicating 'doctrine, movement, system, theory', as in 'Catholicism', 'Marxism' and 'Thatcherism'. It now also indicates 'discrimination', as in 'ageism', 'sexism', 'racism'.

iso- is a prefix indicating 'equal', as in 'isobar', 'isotherm' and 'isosceles'.

-ist is a suffix indicating 'believer, supporter, practitioner', as in 'atheist', 'fascist', 'feminist' and 'Methodist'.

italic type refers to a sloping typeface that is used for a variety of purposes. It is used to differentiate a piece of text from the main text, which is usually in Roman type. For example, it is used sometimes for the titles of books, newspapers, magazines, plays, films, musical works and works of art, as in 'he is a regular reader of *The Times*', 'She reads *Private Eye*', 'Have you read *Animal Farm* by George Orwell', 'He has never seen a production of Shakespeare's *Othello*', 'We went to hear Handel's *Messiah*', '*Mona Lisa* is a famous painting'. Sometimes such titles are put in quotation marks rather than in italic.

Italic type is also sometimes used for the names of ships, trains, etc, as in 'the launch of *The Queen Elizabeth II*', 'She once sailed in *The Queen Mary*' and 'Their train was called *The Flying Scotsman*'.

Italic type is also used for the Latin names of plants and animals, as in 'of the genus *Lilium*', 'trees of the genus *Pyrus*, *Panthera pardus* and *Canis lupus*.

Italic type is sometimes used for foreign words that have been adopted into the English language but have never been fully integrated . Examples include *bête noire*, *raison d'être*, *inter alia* and *Weltschmerz*.

Italic type can also sometimes be used to draw attention to a particular word, phrase or passage, as in 'How do you pronounce *formidable*?', or to emphasize a word or phrase, as in 'Is he *still* in the same job?'

-ite is a suffix which can indicate 'believer, supporter, practitioner', as in 'Thatcherite' and 'Trotskyite'.

-itis is a suffix indicating 'illness or disease', as in 'bronchitis', 'hepatitis' and 'meningitis'.

its and **it's** are liable to be confused. **Its** is an adjective meaning 'belonging to it', as in 'The house has lost its charm' and 'The dog does not like its kennel'. **It's** means 'it is', as in 'Do you know if it's raining?' and 'It's not fair to expect her to do all the chores'.

-ize *see* **-ise**.

J

jargon refers to the technical or specialist language used among members of a particular profession or area. It is often used as a derogatory term to describe unnecessarily obscure or pretentious language used within a profession and incomprehensible to members of the public who might come into contact with it and require to know what is being talked about. **Jargon** should be avoided in any document or situation involving lay people who have no specialist knowledge of the subject being referred to or of the language associated with it. **Jargon** in some professions easily becomes **goddledegook**.

journalese is a derogatory name for the style of writing and choice of vocabulary supposedly found in newspapers. It is usually the style of writing in tabloid newspapers, such as widespread use of clichés, sensational language and short sentences, that is meant by the term. *See* HEADLINE.

jussive refers to a type of clause or sentence that expresses a command, as in 'Do be quiet! I'm trying to study', 'Let's not bother going to the party. I'm too tired', 'Would you pass me that book' and 'Look at that everybody! The river has broken its banks'.

just is an adverb which indicates that something happened a short time previously. In British English it is usually used with the perfect tense of the verb which it accompanies, as in 'I have just finished work', 'We have just decided to buy a new car', 'You've just missed the bus' and 'She's just passed her driving test'.

In American English **just** usually accompanies the past tense of the verb, and some speakers of British English do also, especially in an informal context, as in 'I just saw a bad accident on the motorway', 'We just noticed that it's snowing' and 'He just left'.

Just has more than meaning. It can also mean 'only' and 'exactly'. In the sense of 'only', care should be taken to position it in the correct place in the sentence. For example, in the sentence 'He drank just two glasses of wine', it means that he drank only two glasses of wine, but in the sentence 'He just drank two glasses of wine' it means that he very recently drank two glasses of wine. To add to the confusion, although people may be careful about the positioning of **just** in formal writing they tend not to be in informal writing or speech. Thus someone could say in reply to the questions 'How much has he had to drink? Is he fit to drive?', 'He just had two glasses of wine', meaning that that was all he had drunk. In speech the meaning is usually obvious from intonation and context.

Just can also be used in the sense of 'only' in such sentences as 'Just Peter went on holiday with his parents. The other children stayed at home' and 'Just one coat was left on the stall. The rest were sold early on'. Again care should be taken to place *just* before the word it refers to in order to avoid ambiguity.

Just can also mean 'exactly', as in 'I see you have a food processor. That's just what I need' and 'Where did you find that cape? That's just what I've been looking for'.

K

kibbutzim is an example of an irregular plural form . Most nouns in English form plurals by adding *-s* or *-es* to the singular form, as in 'book and books' and 'church and churches'. However several words of foreign origin which have been adopted into English but not fully integrated retain the plural form found in the foreign language. **Kibbutz**, meaning a communal settlement in Israel, is one such word. Of Hebrew origin, it retains the plural form **kibbutzim**. In some cases there is a growing tendency for foreign plurals to be anglicized, or to exist alongside an anglicized plural, as in 'thesauruses/thesauri', but this is not yet the case with **kibbutzim**.

kilo- is a prefix indicating 'a thousand', as in 'kilogram', 'kilohertz', 'kilolitre', 'kilometre' and 'kilowatt'.

-kin is a suffix which indicates 'a diminutive or smaller version', as in 'lambkin' and 'mannikin'.

kind as a noun can cause grammatical problems. It is used to refer to a class of people or things. Since it is a 'count' noun, it should take the plural form 'kinds' after words such as 'all' and 'many', as in 'He met all kinds of people when he was travelling round the world', 'We found all kinds of treasure when we were clearing out the attic' and 'We found all kinds of wild flower in the meadows'. A

singular noun should follow 'kinds of', as in 'We found
all kinds of treasure' but it is quite common for people to
use a plural noun instead, as in 'We found all kinds of
treasures'. This is best restricted to informal or spoken
use.

'These' and 'those' are frequently found preceding
kind of, as in 'She doesn't like these kind of cakes' and
'My mother used to make those kind of biscuits' but this
is incorrect and 'this' and 'that' should be used, as in 'I
don't like that kind of joke' and 'My mother prefers this
kind of holiday'.

The use of 'kind of' to mean 'somewhat' or 'rather', as
in 'I'm kind of hungry', 'She's kind of rude to him' and
It's kind of cold in there' should be restricted to informal
speech or dialect. This phrase is sometimes written
'kinda', as in 'We're kinda bored'.

Kind is also used as an adjective meaning 'caring' or
'generous', as in 'A kind old lady lent the children money
to get a bus home', 'It was kind of you to let them borrow
your car' and 'Children should be taught to be kind to animals'.

-kind is a suffix indicating 'a group of people', as in 'hu-
mankind', 'mankind', 'womankind'.

kindly looks like an adverb but it can be either an adverb or
an adjective. As an adverb it means 'in a kind or caring
manner' or 'generously', as in 'They treated us kindly
during our stay', 'Her parents kindly treated us to a meal
in a restaurant' and 'They very kindly offered us a lift'.
The adverb **kindly** is also used in rather an ironic way
when the user is annoyed, as in 'Would you kindly stop

allowing your dog to foul the pavement'. It is also used in the phrase 'not to take kindly to', meaning 'to be unwilling to accept', as in 'The new pupil doesn't take kindly to discipline', 'He won't take kindly to being kept waiting' and 'The candidate was so confident that he is unlikely to take kindly to being rejected'.

Kindly is more common as an adjective and means 'kind, warm, friendly', as in 'a kindly old lady who was always helping her neighbours' and 'She gave the children a kindly smile'.

kneel is one of several verbs in English which have more than one past participle and past tense form. The past participle and past tense can both be either 'kneeled' or 'knelt', as in 'The child knelt in prayer', 'She kneeled before the altar' and 'She had knelt at her dying husband's bedside every night' and 'They had kneeled in supplication before the emperor but he spurned them'. Although both 'knelt' and 'kneeled' are acceptable forms in British English, 'knelt' is the more common form.

L

laid and **lain** are liable to be confused. **Laid** is the past tense and past participle of the verb 'lay', meaning 'to place or put', as in 'She laid the antique vase carefully on the table', 'He laid the new carpet tiles in the hall', 'They have laid the baby on a mat on the floor' and 'We have laid vinyl tiles on the kitchen floor'. **Lain** is the past participle of the verb 'lie', 'to rest in a horizontal position', as in 'Those letters have lain on his desk all week', 'The dead man had lain in the empty house for several days', and 'They had lain on the beach in the midday sun'.

language refers to the means by which human beings communicate using words, as in 'Children acquire language at different rates. Some speak much earlier than others'. **Language** can refer either to spoken or written communication. It can also refer to the variety of communication used by a particular nation or state, as in 'He visits France regularly but makes no attempt to understand the French language', 'He won't start to learn a foreign language until he goes to secondary school' and 'People in other parts of Europe tend to speak more languages than the British'. The language that a person speaks from birth is known as his/her 'first language' or 'mother tongue'. He/she is said to be a native speaker of this language.

Language can also be used to refer to the style and vocabulary of a piece of writing, as in 'The language of his novels is very poetic'.

Language can also apply to the particular style and variety of language that is used in a particular profession or among a particular group of people with some common interest, as in 'legal language', 'scientific language', 'technical language', etc. Such technical or specialist language is sometimes referred to rather pejoratively as 'jargon' or as 'legalese', 'medicalese', 'computerese', etc.

A person's own style of **language** with regard to vocabulary, structure, etc, is known as 'ideolect', as in 'He is the son of academic parents and has rather a formal ideolect'.

The **language** of a region or community with regard to vocabulary, structure, grammar and pronunciation is known as 'dialect', as in 'the dialect of the North-East of England'.

last can be an adverb or an adjective. As an adjective it can give rise to ambiguity. It can mean 'coming after all others, final', as in 'He was the last runner to hit the finishing tape', 'That was the last novel he wrote before he died', 'He did not die until he was 90 but he wrote his last novel at the age of 40'. Ambiguity arises when **last** takes on other meanings. For example, it is frequently used as a synonym for 'latest', as in 'I really enjoyed his last novel and I'm looking forward to the next'. In this particular sentence it is clear that **last** means 'latest' not 'final' but this is not always the case. For example, in the sentence 'He was 60 when he directed his last film', it is not at all

clear from the evidence of the sentence alone whether it i
his 'final' or 'latest' film that is being referred to. Thus i
is better to use either 'final' or 'latest' rather than 'last' i
order to clarify the meaning.

Confusion can arise also between **last** meaning 'final
and **last** meaning 'preceding', as in 'I did not quite under
stand the last chapter'. On the evidence of the sentence
alone, it is not clear whether **last** refers to the preceding
chapter or to the final chapter. Again it is best to avoid
ambiguity by using a synonym for **last**.

Yet more confusion can be caused with regard to **last**
when it is used to refer to days of the week. It varies from
person to person whether 'last Saturday' refers to the Saturday that has just gone or to the one before that. To some
extent it depends which day of the week it is when the
statement is made. To avoid ambiguity it is best to specify
the date.

Last is also used as an adverb, as in 'They last saw their
father when he was going to war', 'When the family go to
the dentist my brother always wants to go in last' and 'If
you are adding cream to the soup you add it last'. The adverbial use does not suffer from problems of ambiguity.

latest is an adjective that is liable to be confused with **last**-
see LAST. It can also mean 'most up-to-date', 'most fash-
ionable', as in 'the very latest dresses from the Paris de-
signers'. **Latest** is also found in this meaning in the
phrase 'the very latest', as in 'she always dresses in the
very latest'. It can also mean 'most late', the superlative
of 'late' in the sense of 'far on in the day or night', as in
'The latest train which you can get from that station

lay

leaves at ten o' clock'. In this sense **latest** is also found in the phrase 'at the latest' and in the phrase 'at the very latest', meaning 'most late time', as in 'You must arrive at the station at ten o'clock at the latest' and 'The students' essays must be handed in by Friday at the very latest'.

lay and **lie** are liable to be confused. This is because **lay** as well as being a verb in its own right is also one of the principal parts of **lie**—the past tense as in 'They lay on the beach in the sun', 'The books lay on the table gathering dust' and 'She lay on her bed and wept'.

Lay is a transitive verb meaning 'to place or put', as in 'She asked him to lay new tiles in the kitchen' and 'She had to lay down her shopping to open the door'. The principal parts of **lay** are 'lays' (third person singular present), as in 'She always lays the baby on the grass to play'; 'laying' (present participle), as in 'Laying her shopping down she put her key in the lock'; 'laid' (past participle and past tense), as in 'She laid the package on the table' and 'He had laid his car keys on the table and forgotten about them'.

Lie is an intransitive verb whose principlal parts are 'lies' (third person singular present), as in 'Their house lies to the north of the village'; 'lying' (present participle), as in 'Lying on the grass they looked up at the sky'; 'lay' (past tense), as in 'The climbers lay on the summit exhausted'; 'lain' (past participle), as in 'Those books have lain there for weeks'.

Lie has another totally unrelated meaning. It means 'to say or write something that is untrue', as in 'You didn't have to lie about your part in the affair'. The principal

parts of the verb **lie** are 'lies' (third person singula
present), as in 'lies about why he arrives home late fro
work'; 'lying' (present participle), as in 'Lying, he looke
her straight in the face'; 'lied' (past participle and pas
tense), as in 'He lied to his employers about his qualifica
tions' and 'she suddenly realized that he had lied all th
time'.

lean is one of several verbs in English which have tw
forms of the past tense and the past participle, 'leaned
and 'leant', as in 'She leaned over the fence to talk to he
neighbour', 'He leaned over his desk to catch the atten
tion of his colleagues', 'They have leaned over backward
to help her' and 'She has leant down to pick something u
and hurt her back'. The two forms are interchangeable.

leap is one of several verbs in English which have tw
forms of past tense and past participle, 'leaped' an
'leapt', as in 'The children leaped around the park in hig
spirits', 'She leapt up in surprise when she heard th
news', 'She had leaped over a high fence and broken he
leg' and 'The child has leapt over the steam and run off
The two forms are virtually interchangeable but 'leapt' i
more common in British English.

learn is one of several verbs in English which have tw
forms of past tense and past participle, 'learned' an
'learnt', as in 'They learned French at school', 'She learn
to ski in Austria', 'I think the boys have learned their les
son' and 'He had learnt to be grateful for what he wa
given'. The forms are interchangeable. 'Learned' as a pas
tense or past participle should not be confused wit
'learned', the adjective meaning 'erudite, well-read, intel

lectual', as in 'Students filled the lecture hall to listen to the learned professor' and 'The company publishes learned journals'. This adjective is pronounced with two syllables—*ler-nid*—whereas 'learned', the past tense and past participle, is pronounced as one syllable—*lernd*.

ength mark is a mark used in phonetics in relation to a vowel to indicate that it is long. This can take the form of a 'macron', a small horizontal stroke placed above a letter, or a symbol resembling a colon placed after a vowel in the IPA pronunciation system.

less is a suffix meaning 'without, lacking' added to nouns to form adjectives, as in 'characterless', 'clueless', 'expressionless', 'fearless', 'flawless', 'harmless', 'homeless', 'hopeless', 'passionless', 'toothless' and 'useless'. It can also mean 'without being able to be measured', as in 'ageless', 'countless', 'priceless' and 'timeless'.

ess and **fewer** are liable to be confused. *See* FEWER.

let is a suffix indicating a diminutive or smaller form of something, as in 'booklet', 'coverlet', 'droplet', 'islet', 'piglet', 'starlet' and 'streamlet'.

etter-writing has become something of a dying art in view of the widespread use of the telephone. However, all of us from time to time have to write some form of letter and many of these are business letters. There are a few conventions in formal letters that should be observed.

One's own address, including one's postcode, should be placed at the right-hand side of the page. Each line of one's own address should be indented slightly below the one above and the date put below the last line of the address, as in:

23 Park Driv
Raleig
Blackshir
RA14 2T

5 June 199

Whether one puts a comma at the end of the variou lines of the address is a matter of taste. It is becomin, common in modern usage not to do so.

One's telephone number can either be placed betwee the postcode and the date or at the other side of the pag on the same line as the first line of the address.

If one is writing a business letter one should also put th address of the person to whom one is writing. It should b placed at the other side of the page below one's own ad dress and the lines of this should be placed directly belov each other without being indented, as in:

23, Park Driv
Raleig
Blackshir
RA 14 2T

5 June 1993

The Manager Eastlands Bank
33 West Street
Northlands
Blackshire
NR15 3RJ.

With regard to deciding how to address the person to whom one is writing it is best to find out his/her name. Having done so then one can start the letter off, as in :

Dear Mr White,

If one is writing to a woman the situation is slightly more problematic. Formerly it was considered acceptable to address the person written to as 'Miss' if one knew her to be unmarried or as 'Mrs' if one knew her to be married. If one did not know her marital status one could either use 'Miss' or use the 'Madam' convention. In modern usage 'Ms' is the acceptable term if one does not know the marital status of the woman to whom one is writing. Many people prefer to use this designation even if they do know the person's marital status and many women prefer to be addressed in this way. On the other hand, some women, especially older women, do not like the 'Ms' designation.

In modern usage some people prefer to put the first name and surname of the relevant person instead of the surname preceded by Mr, etc, as in:

Dear John White,

The above style of address is considered rather informal by some people.

If it is not easy to ascertain the name of the person to whom one wishes to write then it is perfectly acceptable to address him/her in terms of their position or job, as in:

Dear manager,

Dear Personnel Manager,

Dear Area Manager,

In formal letters it is also acceptable to use 'Sir' o 'Madam', as in:

Dear Sir,

Dear Madam,

Dear Sir/Madam,

Obviously the above style of address is used in case where one does not know the sex of the person to whom one is writing.

In ending a formal letter it was traditionally the custom to write 'Yours faithfully' before one's signature, if on had addressed the person written to as 'Dear sir' or 'Dea madam', as in :

Yours faithfully
Jane Black

It was also the custom to end the letter with 'Yours sin cerely' if the letter was either informal in nature or a for mal letter which began with 'Dear Mr White' etc, as in:

Yours sincerely
Mary Brown

In modern usage it is now considered acceptable to en a letter with 'Yours sincerely' even if one has begun i with 'Dear sir', etc. 'Yours faithfully' is considered ex ceptionally formal.

It is common to end even business letters with 'Kind re gards', especially if the person written to is known to one

On the envelope the lines can be indented or not, according to taste. Each line, except the last one, can have a comma after or not. However, in modern usage there is an increasing tendency to punctuate as little as possible and the commas are frequently omitted, as in:

Ms Mary Brown
29 Lower Forth Street
Redwood
Blackshire
RD16 5YP.

The same comments on Mrs, Miss and Ms apply to envelopes as apply to the opening greeting in letters. *See above*. Anything that can be done to make the address as clear as possible should be done. It is important always to put the postcode as failure to do so slows down delivery of the letter. It is also advisable to highlight the town one is sending the letter to, either by putting it in capital letters, or by underlining it, as in:

Mr James Green
45, Park Avenue
BOSTON
Blackshire
BT16 6GH.

In modern usage it is becoming increasingly common to write the full name of the person written to on the envelope, as in:

James Black
36, High Street
BLANKTON
Blankshire
BL13 9T2.

It is considered formal or old-fashioned to use 'Esq.
usually spelt with a full stop at the end and preceded by
comma. If used, 'Esq.' should be placed after the mans
name and there should be no accopmanying 'Mr', as in:

John Brown, Esq
43 Queen Street
Whiteoaks
Blankshire
WH12 TY.

lexicography refers to the art and practice of definin
words, selecting them and arranging them in dictionari
and glossaries.

licence and **license** are liable to be confused. **Licence** is
noun referring to 'a document indicating that official pe
mission or authorization has been given to do something
as in 'He does not have a current driving licence', 'Yc
need a trading licence to sell goods there' and 'The pu
owner lost his licence'. **Licence** also means 'too gre
freedom, disregard for rules of behaviour, social accep
ability, morals, etc', as in 'The organizers of the conce
objected to the licence shown by the young people in the
dress'. In this sense the word **licence** is usually used
formal situations.

  License is a verb meaning 'to give a licence to, to gi

official permission or authorization to', as in 'He is licensed to sell alcohol', 'She is not licensed to sell goods in the market' and 'The restaurant is not licensed but you can bring your own wine'. **Licence** is often misspelt as **license**.

The above comments refer to British English. In American English **license** is used for both the noun and the verb.

ie *see* **lay**.

ligature refers to a printed character combining two letters in one, as in æ and œ. It is sometimes called a 'digraph'.

like is a suffix indicating similarity, as in 'childlike', 'cowlike', 'dreamlike', 'ladylike', 'lifelike' and 'warlike'.

ling is a suffix indicating a diminutive or smaller version of something, as in 'duckling', 'gosling' and 'nestling'.

logue is a suffix derived from Greek meaning 'indicating 'conversation, discussion', as in 'dialogue', 'epilogue', 'monologue', 'prologue' and 'travelogue'.

limerick refers to a humorous five-lined piece of light verse, with the first two lines rhyming with each other, the third and fourth lines rhyming with each other, and the fifth line rhyming with the first line. Usually there are three stressed beats in the first, second and fifth lines and two stressed beats on the third and fourth lines. Traditionally the name of a place is mentioned in the first line and may be repeated in the last line. Edward Lear made the form popular in the nineteenth century. Limerick is a town in Ireland but the name of the verse is probably derived from a Victorian custom of singing nonsense songs at parties where 'Will you come up to Limerick' was a common refrain. An example is:

There once was a man from Nantucket
Who kept all his cash in a bucket;
   But his daughter named Nan
   Ran away with a man,
And as for the bucket, Nantucket.

lingua franca refers to 'a language adopted as a common language by speakers whose mother tongues or native languages are different'. This enables people to have a common medium of communication for various purposes, such as trading. Examples include Swahili in East Africa, Hausa in West Africa and Tok Pisin in Papua New Guinea. The term historically referred to 'a language that was a mixture of Italian, French, Greek, Spanish and Arabic, used for trading and military purposes.'

linguistics refers to the systematic, scientific study of language. It describes language and seeks to establish general principles rather than to prescribe rules of correctness.

line-break refers to the division of a word at the end of a line for space purposes. This is marked by a 'hyphen'. *See* HYPHEN.

linking adverbs and **linking adverbials** refer to words and phrases which indicate some kind of connection between one clause or sentence and another. Examples include 'however', as in 'The award had no effect on their financial situation. It did, however, have a marked effect on their morale'; 'moreover', as in 'He is an unruly pupil. Moreover, he is a bad influence on the other pupils'; 'then again', as in 'She does not have very good qualifications. Then again, most of the other candidates have even fewer'; 'in the meantime', as in 'We will not know the planning committee's decision until next week. In the meantime we can only hope'; 'instead', as in 'I thought he would have reigned. Instead he seems determined to stay'.

inking verb is a verb which 'links' a subject with its complement. Unlike other verbs, **linking verbs** do not denote an action but indicate a state. Examples of **linking verbs** include 'He is a fool', 'She appears calm', 'He appeared a sensible man', 'You seemed to become anxious', 'They became Buddhists', 'The child feels unwell', 'It is getting rather warm', 'It is growing colder', 'You look well', 'She remained loyal to her friend', 'She lived in America but remained a British citizen' and 'You seem thoughtful' and 'She seems a nice person'. **Linking verbs** are also called 'copula' or 'copular verbs'.

terary criticism refers to the formal study, discussion and evaluation of a literary work, as in 'The students who are studying literary criticism have been asked to write a critical analysis of *Ulysses* by James Joyce.'

totes refers to a kind of understatement in which a statement is conveyed by contradicting or denying its opposite, as in 'It will be no easy task to look after their children for a week' (meaning that it will be a difficult task), 'She's not exactly communicative' (meaning she is silent or reserved).

anword refers to a word that has been taken into another language from another. From the point of view of the language taking the word in, the word is known as a 'borrowing'—*see* BORROWING. Some **loanwords** become naturalized or fully integrated into the language and have a pronunciation and spelling reflecting the conventions of the language which has borrowed it. Other **loanwords** retain the spelling and pronunciation of the language from which they have been borrowed. These include 'Gastarbeiter', borrowed from German and meaning 'a foreign worker'.

localism refers to a word or expression whose use is restricted to a particular place or area. The area in question can be quite small, unlike 'dialect' words or 'regionalism'.

lower-case letter is the opposite of 'capital letter'. It is also known informally as 'small letter'. **Lower-case letters** are used for most words in the language. It is 'capital letters' which are exceptional in their use. *See* CAPITAL LETTER.

-ly is a common adverbial ending. *See* ADVERBS.

M

macro- is a prefix derived from the Greek meaning 'large in size or scope', as in 'macrobiotic', 'macrocosm', 'macroeconomics', 'macromolecular' and 'macrostructure'.

macron *see* **length mark**.

main clause refers to the principal clause in a sentence on which any 'subordinate clauses' depend for their sense. The main clause can stand alone and make some sense but the subordinate clauses cannot. In the sentence 'I left early because I wanted to catch the 6 o'clock train', 'I left early' is the principal clause and 'because I wanted to catch the 6 o'clock train' is the subordinate clause. In the sentence 'When we saw the strange man we were afraid', the main clause is 'we were afraid' and the subordinate clause is 'when we saw the strange man'. In the sentence 'Because it was late we decided to start out for home as soon as we could', the main clause is 'we decided to start out for home' and the subordinate clauses are 'because it was late' and 'as soon as we could'. A **main clause** can also be known as a 'principal clause' or an 'independent clause'.

mal- is a prefix derived from French meaning 'bad, unpleasant', as in 'malodorous', or 'imperfect, faulty', as in 'malabsorption', 'maladjusted', 'maladministration' 'malformation', 'malfunctioning', 'malnutrition', 'ma practice' and 'maltreatment'.

malapropism refers to the incorrect use of a word, ofter through confusion with a similar-sounding word. It ofter arises from someone's attempt to impress someone els with a knowledge of long words or of technical language Examples include 'The doctor says the old man is not i possession of all his facilities'. Here 'facilities' has bee wrongly used instead of 'faculties'. Another example i 'My friend lives in a computer belt'. Here 'computer' ha been wrongly used instead of 'commuter'. Another exam ple is 'Her husband's had a vivisection'. Here 'vivisec tion' has been used instead of 'vasectomy'. 'Ah! It's won derful to be on terracotta again. I hate sailing'. Her 'terracotta' has been wrongly used instead of 'terr firma'. The effect of **malapropism** is often humorou Sometimes people use it deliberately for a comic effec as in 'He was under the affluence of incahol'.

Malapropism is called after Mrs Malaprop, a characte in a play called *The Rivals* (1775), a comedy by R. E Sheridan. Her name is derived from the French *mal à propo* 'not apposite, inappropriate'. Some of her **malapropisms** i the play include 'She's as headstrong as an allegory on th banks of the Nile'. She has used 'allegory' wrongly ii stead of 'alligator'. Another of Mrs Malapropism's **mala propisms** is 'Illiterate him quite from your mind'. Her she has used 'illiterate' wrongly instead of 'obliterate'.

major sentence can be used to refer to a sentence that co tains at least one subject and a finite verb, as in 'We a going' and 'They won'. They frequently have more elements than this, as in 'They bought a car', 'We lost the match', 'They arrived yesterday' and 'We are going away next week'. They are sometimes described as 'regular' because they divide into certain structural patterns, a subject, finite verb, adverb or adverbial, etc. The opposite of a **major sentence** is called a 'minor sentence', 'irregular sentence' or 'fragmentary sentence'. These include interjections such as 'Ouch!' and 'How terrible'; formula expressions, such as 'Good morning' and 'Well done'; and short forms of longer expressions, as in 'Traffic diverted', 'Shop closed', 'No dogs' and 'Flooding ahead'. Such short forms could be rephrased to become 'major sentences', as in 'Traffic has been diverted because of roadworks', 'The shop is closed on Sundays', 'The owner does not allow dogs in her shop' and 'There was flooding ahead on the motorway'.

man is used with nouns to form nouns indicating someone's job, as in 'barman', 'chairman', 'clergyman', 'coalman', 'fireman', 'policeman', 'postman', 'salesman'. In modern usage when attempts are being made to remove sexism from the language alternatives have been sought for any words ending in **-man**. Formerly, words ending in **-man** were often used whether or not the person referred to was definitely known to be a man. Different ways have been found to avoid the sexism of **-man**. 'Salesman' has been changed in many cases to 'salesperson', 'chairman' often becomes 'chairperson' or 'chair'. Similarly, 'fireman' has become 'fire-fighter' and 'policeman' frequently becomes 'police officer'. *See* -PERSON.

-mania is a suffix indicating abnormal or obsessional be
haviour, as in 'kleptomania', 'nymphomania' and 'pyro
mania'.

manner, adverbs of *see* **adverb**.

manner, adverbial clause of *see* **adverbial clause**.

masculine in grammatical terms refers to one of the gram
matical genders that nouns are divided into. Nouns in the
masculine gender include words that obviously belong to
the male sex, as in 'man', 'boy', 'king', 'prince' 'bride
groom', 'schoolboy' and 'salesman'. Many words now
considered to be 'of dual gender' formerly were assumed
to be masculine. These include such words as 'author'
'sculptor' and 'engineer'. *See* GENDER. Gender also ap
plies to personal pronouns and the third personal singular
pronoun masculine is 'he' (subject), 'him' (object) and
'his' (possessive). For further information *see* HE; SHE.

mass noun is the same as UNCOUNTABLE NOUN.

-mate is a suffix referring to 'someone who shares some
thing with someone', as in 'bedmate', 'classmate', 'room
mate', 'schoolmate', 'shipmate', 'team-mate' and 'work
mate'.

mega- is a prefix derived from Greek meaning 'very large'
as in 'megabid', 'megabucks', 'megaproduction' and
'megastar'. Many words using **mega-** in this way are
modern and many of them are also informal or slang. In
technical language **mega-** means 'a million times bigger
than the unit to which it is attached, as in 'megabyte'
'megacycle', 'megahertz' and 'megawatt'.

meiosis is a figure of speech using understatement to empha
size the size or importance of something, as in 'He's a decen

enough bloke' and 'He's rather a decent tennis player'.

melted and **molten** are liable to be confused. **Melted** is the past tense and past participle of the verb 'to melt', as in 'The chocolate melted in the heat' and 'The ice cream had melted by the time they got home'. **Melted** is also used as an adjective, as in 'melted chocolate'. **Molten** is used only as an adjective but it is not synonymous with **melted**. It means 'melted or made liquid at high temperatures', as in 'molten lava' and 'molten metal'.

meta- is a prefix derived from Greek indicating 'alteration or transformation', as in 'metamorphosis', 'metaphor' and 'metaphysics'.

metaphor is a figure of speech which compares two things by saying that one thing is another, as in 'He was a lion in the fight' (meaning that he was as brave as a lion), 'She is a mouse whenever he is present' (meaning that she is very timid), 'He is a giant among men' (meaning that he is a great man), 'She was a shining light to us all' (meaning she was a source of inspiration) and 'Life was not a bed of roses' (meaning life was not easy and enjoyable). By extension, **metaphor** refers to a word or phrase used in a sentence where it does not have a literal meaning, as in 'a butter mountain', 'a wine lake', 'My colleague is a snake in the grass', 'She always sits on the fence at committee meetings', They walked home with leaden feet' and 'He was rooted to the spot when he saw the man with the gun'. *See* MIXED METAPHOR and SIMILE.

meter is a suffix indicating 'a measuring instrument', as in 'altimeter', 'barometer', 'pedometer', 'calorimeter', 'speedometer', 'thermometer'.

metonym is a figure of speech in which a word or expression is used to indicate something with which it has
close relationship, as in 'The position of the Crown i
more uncertain than it was formerly' (meaning that th
position of the monarchy is not as stable as it once was
'The City is nervously awaiting the announcement of thi
month's trade figures' (meaning that the people who wor
in London's financial sector are nervously awaiting th
announcement of this month's trade figures) and 'Th
Kremlin began to adopt a more enlightened approach t
foreign visitors' (meaning that the Russian governme
began to adopt a more enlightened approach to foreig
visitors), 'The White house has yet to comment on th
proposal' (meaning that the President of the United State
has yet to reply to the proposal).

-metre is a suffix indicating 'meter, the unit of length', as i
'centimetre', 'kilometre' and 'millimetre'.

micro- is a prefix derived from Greek meaning 'ver
small', as in 'microbiology', 'microfiche', 'microfilm
'microscope', 'microsurgery'.

milli- is a prefix derived from Latin meaning 'thousand', a
in 'millisecond'.

mini- is a prefix derived from Latin meaning 'very smal
least', as in 'minimum', 'minimal', and 'miniature'
Mini- is frequently used to form modern words, as i
'minibus', 'minicab', 'mini-computer', 'mini-cruise'
'mini-golf', 'mini-market' and 'miniskirt'. Moder
words beginning with **mini-** can be spelt either with a hy
phen or without.

minor sentence *see* **major sentence**.

mis- is a prefix indicating 'badly, wrongly', as in 'misbe-
have', 'miscalculate', 'misdirect', 'mishandle', 'mishear',
'misjudge', 'mismanage', 'mispronounce', 'misspell',
'mistreat', 'mistrust', 'misunderstanding' and 'misuse'.

mixed metaphor occurs when unrelated metaphors are put
in the same sentence. Examples include 'She sailed into
the room with both guns blazing'. Here the use of the
word 'sail' belongs to nautical metaphors but the 'guns
blazing' belongs to cowboy or Wild West metaphors. Another example is 'The company's new flagship did not get
off the ground'. Here 'flagship' is a nautical term and 'get
off the ground' refers to aircraft'. Another example is
'They were caught red-handed with their trousers down'.
Here 'caught red-handed' is a metaphorical reference to a
murderer caught with blood on his/her hands but 'caught
with one's trousers down' is either a reference to the embarrassing experience of being caught unawares in the
toilet or else caught in an embarrassing sexual situation.

modifier refers to a word, or group of words, that 'modifies' or affects the meaning of another word in some way,
usually by adding more information about it. **Modifiers**
are frequently used with nouns. They can be adjectives, as
in 'He works in the *main* building' and 'They need a
larger house'. **Modifiers** of nouns can be nouns themselves, as in 'the *theatre* profession', 'the *publishing* in-
dustry' and '*singing* tuition'. They can also be place
names, as in 'the *Edinburgh* train', 'a *Paris* cafe' and 'the
London underground' or adverbs of place and direction,
as in 'a *downstairs* cloakroom' and 'an *upstairs* sitting
room.

Adverbs, adjectives and pronouns can be accompanied by **modifiers.** Examples of modifiers with adverbs include 'walking *amazingly* quickly' and 'stopping *incredibly* abruptly'. Examples of modifiers with adjectives include 'a *really* warm day' and 'a *deliriously* happy child'. Examples of modifiers with pronouns include '*almost* no one there' and '*practically* everyone present'.

The examples given above are all 'pre-modifiers'. *See also* POST-MODIFIER.

-monger is a suffix derived from Old English meaning 'dealer, trader', as in 'fishmonger' and 'ironmonger'. As well as being used for occupations in which people sell things, it is used for people who 'trade' in less tangible things, as in 'gossipmonger', 'rumourmonger', 'scaremonger' and 'warmonger'.

mono- is a prefix derived from Greek meaning 'one, single', as in 'monochrome', 'monocracy', 'monogamy', 'monologue', 'monoplane', 'monosyllabic' and 'monoxide'.

months of the year are spelt with initial capital letters, as in January, February, March, April, May, June, July, August, September, October, November and December.

modal verb refers to a type of 'auxiliary verb' that 'helps' the main verb to express a range of meanings including, for example, such meanings as possibility, probability, wants, wishes, necessity, permission, suggestions, etc. The main modal verbs are 'can', 'could'; 'may', 'might'; 'will', 'would'; 'shall', 'should'; 'must'. Modal verbs have only one form. They have no -*s* form in the third person singular, no infinitive and no participles. Examples of

mood

modal verbs include 'He cannot read and write', 'She could go if she wanted to' (expressing ability); 'You can have another biscuit', 'You may answer the question' (expressing permission); 'We may see her on the way to the station', 'We might get there by nightfall' (expressing possibility); 'Will you have some wine?', 'Would you take a seat?' (expressing an offer or invitation); 'We should arrive by dawn', 'That must be a record' (expressing probability and certainty); 'You may prefer to wait', 'You might like to leave instructions' (expressing suggestion); 'Can you find the time to phone him for me?' ,'Could you give him a message?' (expressing instructions and requests); 'They must leave at once', 'We must get there on time' (expressing necessity).

mood refers to one of the categories into which verbs are divided. The verb moods are 'indicative', 'imperative' and 'subjunctive'. The indicative makes a statement, as in 'He lives in France', 'They have two children' and 'It's starting to rain'. The 'imperative' is used for giving orders or making requests, as in 'Shut that door!', 'Sit quietly until the teacher arrives' and 'Please bring me some coffee'. The subjunctive was originally a term in Latin grammar and expressed a wish, supposition, doubt, improbability or other non-factual statement. It is used in English for hypothetical statements and certain formal 'that' clauses, as in 'If I were you I would have nothing to do with it', 'If you were to go now you would arrive on time', 'Someone suggested that we ask for more money' and 'It was his solicitor who suggested that he sue the firm'. The word **mood** arose because it was said to indicate the verb's attitude or viewpoint. *See* SUBJUNCTIVE.

more is an adverb which is added to some adjectives to make the comparative form. In general it is the longer adjectives which have **more** as part of their comparative form, as in 'more abundant', 'more beautiful', 'more catastrophic', 'more dangerous', 'more elegant', 'more frantic', 'more graceful', 'more handsome', 'more intelligent', 'more luxurious', 'more manageable', 'more noteworthy', 'more opulent', 'more precious', 'more ravishing', 'more satisfactory', 'more talented', 'more unusual', 'more valuable'. Examples of adverbs with **more** in their comparative form include 'more elegantly', 'more gracefully', 'more energetically', 'more dangerously' and 'more determinedly'. *See* COMPARISON OF ADJECTIVES.

most is an adverb added to some adjectives and adverbs to make the superlative form. In general it is the longer adjectives which have **most** as part of their superlative form, as in 'most abundant', 'most beautiful', 'most catastrophic', 'most dangerous', 'most elegant', 'most frantic', 'most graceful', 'most handsome', 'most intelligent', 'most luxurious', 'most manageable', 'most noteworthy', 'most opulent', 'most precious', most ravishing', 'most satisfactory', 'most talented', 'most unusual', 'most valuable'. Examples of adverbs with **most** in their superlative form include 'most elegantly', 'most gracefully', 'most energetically', 'most dangerously' and 'most determinedly'.

mother tongue refers to the language that one first learns, the language of which one is a 'native speaker'. It means the same as 'native tongue'.

ns, miss and miss *see* **letter-writing**.

mow has two possible past participles—**mowed and mown**, as in 'He has not yet mowed the grass' and 'We have mown the grass several times this summer'. The two participles are interchangeable. Only **mowed**, however, can be used as the past tense, as in 'They mowed the grass yesterday' and 'If they mowed the grass more often the garden would be tidier'. **Mown** can also be an adjective, as in 'the smell of freshly mown hay'.

multi- is a prefix derived from Latin meaning 'many many', as in 'multiply', 'multitude' and 'multitudinous'. **Multi-** is frequently used to form new modern words, as in 'multi-married', 'multi-media', 'multi-publicized', 'multi-purpose', 'multi-storey ', 'multi-talented' and 'multi-travelled'.

multi-sentence refers to a sentence with more than one clause, as in 'She tripped over a rock and broke her ankle' and 'She was afraid when she saw the strange man'.

N

-naut is a suffix derived from Greek 'sailor' and meanin
'navigator', as in 'astronaut' and 'cosmonaut'.

negative sentence refers to a sentence that is the opposit
of 'positive sentence'. 'She has a dog' is an example of
positive sentence. 'She does not have a dog' is an exam
ple of a **negative sentence**. The **negative** concept is ex
pressed by an 'auxiliary' verb accompanied by 'not' c
'n't'. Other words used in **negative sentences** includ
'never', 'nothing' and 'by no means', as in 'She has neve
been here' and 'We heard nothing'.

neither as an adjective or a pronoun takes a singular verb
as in 'Neither parent will come' and 'Neither of ther
wishes to come'. In the **neither ... nor** construction,
singular verb is used if both parts of the construction ar
singular, as in 'Neither Jane nor Mary was present'. I
both parts are plural the verb is plural, as in 'Neither the
parents nor their grandparents are willing to look afte
them'. If the construction involves a mixture of singula
and plural, the verb traditionally agrees with the subje
that is nearest it, as in 'Neither her mother nor her grand
parents are going to come' and 'Neither her grandparent
nor her mother is going to come'. If pronouns are use

the nearer one governs the verb as in 'Neither they nor he is at fault' and 'Neither he nor they are at fault'.

neologism refers to a word that has been newly coined or newly introduced into the language, as 'camcorder', 'Jacuzzi' and 'karaoke'.

neuro- is a prefix derived from Greek meaning 'nerve', as in 'neuritis', 'neurology', 'neuron' and 'neurosurgery'.

neuter refers to one of the grammatical genders. The other two grammatical genders are 'masculine' and 'feminine'. Inanimate objects are members of the **neuter** gender. Examples include 'table', 'desk', 'garden', 'spade', 'flower' and 'bottle'.

non-finite clause is a clause which contains a 'non-finite verb'. Thus in the sentence 'He works hard to earn a living', 'to earn a living' is a non-finite clause since 'to earn' is an infinitive and so a non-finite verb. Similarly in the sentence 'Getting there was a problem', 'getting there' is a non-finite clause, 'getting' being a present participle and so a non-finite verb.

non-finite verb is one which shows no variation in tense and which has no subject. The non-finite verb forms include the infinitive form, as in 'go', the present participle and gerund, as in 'going', and the past participle, as in 'gone'.

noun indicates the name of something or someone. Thus 'anchor', 'baker', 'cat', 'elephant', 'foot', 'gate', 'lake', 'pear', 'shoe', 'trunk' and 'wallet' are all nouns. There are various categories of nouns. *See* ABSTRACT NOUN, COMMON NOUN, CONCRETE NOUN, COUNTABLE NOUN, PROPER NOUN and UNCOUNTABLE NOUN.

noun clause refers to a 'subordinate clause' which performs a function in a sentence similar to a noun or noun phrase. It can act as the subject, object or complement of main clause. In the sentence 'Where he goes is his own business', 'where he goes' is a **noun clause**. In the sentence 'They asked why he objected', 'why he objected' is a **noun clause**. A **noun clause** is also known as a **nominal clause**.

noun phrase refers to a group of words containing a noun as its main word and functioning like a noun in a sentence. Thus it can function as the subject, object or complement of a sentence. In the sentence 'The large black dog bit him', 'the large black dog' is a **noun phrase** and in the sentence 'They bought a house with a garden' 'with a garden' is a **noun phrase**. In the sentence 'She is complete fool', 'a complete fool' is a noun phrase.

number in grammar is a classification consisting of 'singular' and 'plural'. Thus the **number** of the pronoun 'they' is 'plural' and the **number** of the verb 'carries' is singular. *See* NUMBER AGREEMENT.

number agreement or **concord** refers to the fact that grammatical units should agree in terms of number. Thus a singular subject is followed by a singular verb, as in 'The girl likes flowers', 'He hates work' and 'She was carrying suitcase'. Similarly a plural subject should be followed by a plural verb, as in 'They have many problems', 'The men work hard' and 'The girls are training hard'.

numbers can be written in either figures or words. It is largely a matter of taste which method is adopted. As long as the method is consistent it does not really matter. Some establishments, such as a publishing house or a newspaper office, will have a house style. For example, some of them prefer to have numbers up to 10 written in words, as in 'They have two boys and three girls'. If this system is adopted, guidance should be sought as to whether a mixture of figures and words in the same sentence is acceptable, as in 'We have 12 cups but only six saucers', or whether the rule should be broken in such situations as 'We have twelve cups but only six saucers'.

numeral is a word for 'number', as in 'print all the numerals in bold type'. **Numeral** is often used to refer to 'one, two, three, etc' in grammar since **number** is used to refer to the singular/plural category.

O

object refers to the part of a sentence that is acted upon or is affected by the verb. It usually follows the verb to which it relates. There are two forms of **object**—the 'direct object' and 'indirect object'. A direct object can be a noun, and in the sentence 'The girl hit the ball', 'ball' is a noun and the object. In the sentence 'They bought a house', 'house' is a noun and the object. In the sentence 'They made an error', 'error' is a noun and the object. A direct object can be a noun phrase, and in the sentence 'He has bought a large house', 'a large house' is a noun phrase and the object. In the sentence 'She loves the little girl', 'the little girl' is a noun phrase and the object. In the sentence 'They both wear black clothes', 'black clothes' is a noun phrase and the object'. A direct object can be a noun clause, and in the sentence 'I know what he means', 'what he means' is a noun phrase and the object. In the sentence 'He denied that he had been involved', 'that he had been involved' is a noun phrase and the object. In the sentence 'I asked when he would return', 'when he would return' is a noun phrase and the object. A direct object can also be a pronoun, and in the sentence 'She hit him', 'him' is a pronoun and the object. In the sentence 'They had a car but they sold it', 'it' is a pronoun and the object. In the sentence 'She loves them', 'them' is a pronoun and the object. *See* INDIRECT OBJECT.

objective case is the case expressing the 'object' . In Latin it is known as the 'accusative' case.

oblique is a diagonal mark / which has various uses. Its principal use is to show alternatives, as in 'he/she', 'Dear Sir/Madam', 'two/three-room flat' and 'the budget for 1993/4'. The **oblique** is used in some abbreviations, as in ' c/o Smith' (meaning 'care of Smith'). The word 'per' is usually shown by means of an **oblique**, as in 60km/hr (60 kilometres per hour).

officialese is a derogatory term for the vocabulary and style of writing often found in official reports and documents and thought of as being pretentious and difficult to understand. It is usually considered to be the prime example of GOBBLEDEGOOK.

-oholic *see* **-aholic**.

-ology is a suffix derived from Greek indicating 'study of', as in 'biology', 'geology' and 'technology'.

omni- is a prefix derived from Latin indicating 'all', as in 'omnipotent' and 'omnivorous'.

onomatopoeia is a figure of speech which uses words whose sound suggests their meaning, as in 'The sausages sizzled in the pan', 'The fire crackled in the grate' and 'The water gurgled in the pipes'.

orthographic refers to spelling, as in 'words which give rise to orthographic problems'.

orthography means the study or science of how words are spelt, as in 'make a survey of the orthography and the pronunciation of Scandinavian languages'.

ordinal numbers refer to 'first', 'second', 'third', etc, as opposed to 'cardinal numbers' which are 'one', 'two', 'three', etc.

-osis is a suffix derived from Greek indicating either 'a disease', as in 'cirrhosis' and 'thrombosis'.

oxymoron is a figure of speech which is based on the linking of incongruous or contradictory words, as in 'and honour rooted in dishonour stood' (Tennyson) and 'the wisest fool in Christendom'.

P

paragraph is a subdivision of a piece of prose. Many people find it difficult to divide their work into paragraphs. Learning to do so can be difficult but it is an area of style that improves with practice and writers develop an intuition as when to start a new paragraph.

A **paragraph** should deal with one particular theme or point of the writer's writing or argument. When that has been dealt with, a new paragraph should be started.

However, there are other considerations to be taken into account. If the paragraph is very long it can appear offputting visually to the would-be reader and can be difficult to make one's way through as a reader. In such cases it is best to sub-divide one's themes and shorten one's paragraphs.

On the other hand it is best not to make all of one's paragraphs too short or this can create a disjointed, rather staccato effect which might well not be intended. It is best to try to aim for a mixture of lengths to create some variety in one's writing and to tempt one's potential readers to read on.

Traditionally it was frowned upon to have a one-sentence paragraph but there are no hard and fast rules about this. Usually it takes more than one sentence to develop the theme of the paragraph, unless one is a tabloid journalist or copywriter for an advertising firm, and it is best to avoid long, complex sentences.

The opening paragraph of a piece of writing should introduce the topic about which one is writing. The closing paragraph should sum up what one has been writing about. New paragraphs begin on new lines and they are usually indented from the margin. In the case of dialogue in a work of fiction, each speaker's utterance usually begins on a new line for the clarification of the reader.

parenthesis *see* **brackets**.

passive voice designates the voice of a verb whereby the subject is the recipient of the action of the verb. Thus, in the sentence 'Mary was kicked by her brother', 'Mary' is the receiver of the 'kick' and so 'kick' is in the passive voice. Similarly, in the sentence 'James was hit by the ball', 'James' is the receiver of the 'hit' and so 'hit' is in the passive voice. Had the former sentence been in the active voice it would have been 'Her brother kicked Mary'. In this sentence 'the brother' is the subject and not the receiver of the action.

past participles are formed by adding *-ed* or *-d* to the base words of regular verbs, as in 'acted', ' alluded', 'boarded', 'dashed', 'flouted', 'handed', 'loathed', 'tended' and 'wanted', or in various other ways for irregular verbs. *See* IRREGULAR VERBS.

past tense is formed by adding *-ed* or *-d* to the base form of the verb in regular verbs, as in 'added', 'crashed', 'graded', 'smiled', 'rested' and 'yielded', and in various ways for irregular verbs. *See* IRREGULAR VERBS and TENSE.

perfect tense *see* **tense**.

period *see* **full stop**.

personal pronouns are used to refer back to someone or something that has already been mentioned. The personal pronouns are divided into subject pronouns, object , pronouns and possessive pronouns. They are also categorized according to 'person'. *See* FIRST PERSON, SECOND PERSON and THIRD PERSON.

plural noun refers to 'more than one' and is contrasted with 'singular noun'. Singular nouns form plural forms in different ways. Most singular nouns add *s*, as in 'bat/bats', 'monkey/monkeys', 'table/tables', 'umbrella/umbrellas', or add *es*, as in 'church/churches' or 'torch/torches'. Singular nouns ending in a consonant followed by *y* add *ies*, as in 'fairy/fairies' and 'story/stories'. Some plural forms are formed irregularly. *See* IRREGULAR PLURALS.

possessive apostrophe *see* **apostrophe**.

possessive pronoun *see* **personal pronoun**, **first person**, **second person** and **third person**.

postmodifiers come after the main word of a noun phrase, as in 'of stone' in 'tablets of stone'.

predicate refers to all the parts of a clause or sentence that are not contained in the subject. Thus in the sentence 'The little girl was exhausted and hungry', 'exhausted and hungry' is the **predicate**. Similarly, in the sentence 'The tired old man slept like a top', 'slept like a top' is the **predicate**.

predicative adjectives help to form the predicate and so come after the verb, as 'tired' in 'She was very tired' and 'mournful' in 'The music was very mournful'.

premodifiers come before the main word of a noun phrase as 'green' in 'green dress' and 'pretty' in 'pretty houses'

prepositions are words which relate two elements of a sentence, clause or phrase together. They show how the elements relate in time or space and generally precede th words which they 'govern'. Words governed by **prepositions** are nouns or pronouns. **Prepositions** are often ver short words, as 'at', 'in', 'on', 'to', 'before' and 'after' Some complex prepositions consist of two words, a 'ahead of', 'instead of', 'apart from', and some consist o three, as 'with reference to', 'in accordance with' and 'i addition to'. Examples of **prepositions** in sentences include 'The cat sat on the mat', 'We were at a concert' 'They are in shock', 'We are going to France', 'She ar rived before me', 'Apart from you she has no friends' an 'We acted in accordance with your instructions'.

present continuous *see* **tense**.

present participle *see* **-ing words**.

present tense *see* **tense**.

pronoun is a word that takes the place of a noun or a nou phrase. *See* PERSONAL PRONOUNS, HE, HER, HIM and HIS, RE CIPROCAL PRONOUNS, REFLEXIVE PRONOUNS, DEMONSTRATIV PRONOUNS, RELATIVE PRONOUNS, DISTRIBUTIVE PRONOUNS, IN DEFINITE PRONOUNS and INTERROGATIVE PRONOUNS.

proper noun is a noun which refers to a particular indi vidual or specific thing. It is the 'name' of someone o something', as in Australia, Vesuvius, John Brown, Rive Thames, Rome and Atlantic Ocean. *See* CAPITAL LETTERS.

Q

question mark refers to the punctuation mark that is placed at the end of a question or interrogative sentence, as in 'Who is he?', 'Where are they?', 'Why have they gone?', 'Whereabouts are they?', 'When are you going?' and 'What did he say?'. The **question mark** is sometimes known as the 'query'.

question tag refers to a phrase that is interrogative in form but is not really asking a question. It is added to a statement to seek agreement, etc. Examples include 'That was a lovely meal, wasn't it?', 'You will be able to go, won't you?', 'He's not going to move house, is he?' and 'She doesn't drive, does she?'. Sentences containing **question tags** have 'question marks' at the end.

query *see* **question mark**.

quotation marks, also known as 'inverted commas' or 'quotes', are used in 'direct speech'. For the use of **quotation marks** in 'direct speech' *see* DIRECT SPEECH. **Quotation marks** are also used to enclose titles of newspapers, books, plays, films, musical works and works of art, as in 'The Times', 'Animal Farm', 'Othello', 'My Fair Lady' and 'Portrait of the Artist'. **Quotation marks** may consist of a set of single inverted comas or a set of double inverted commas. If a title, etc, is to be enclosed in quotation

marks and the title is part of a piece of writing already
quotation marks for some other reason, such as being p.
of direct speech, then the quotation marks round the ti
should be in the type of quotation marks opposite to t
other ones. Thus if the piece of writing is in single quot
tion marks then the title should be in double quotati
marks. If the piece of prose is in double quotation mar
the title should be in single quotation marks. Exampl
include 'Have you read "Wuthering Heights"?' and "D
you go to see 'My Fair Lady'?"

quotes *see* **quotation marks**.

R

re- is a common prefix, meaning 'again', in verbs. In most cases it is not followed by a hyphen, as in 'retrace one's footsteps', 'a retrial ordered by the judge' and 'reconsider his decision'. However, it should be followed by a hyphen if its absence is likely to lead to confusion with another word, as in 're-cover a chair'/'recover from an illness', 're-count the votes'/'recount a tale of woe', 'the re-creation of a 17th-century village for a film set'/'play tennis for recreation' and 're-form the group'/'reform the prison system'. In cases where the second element of a word begins with *e*, **re-** is traditionally followed by a hyphen, as in 're-educate', 're-entry' and 're-echo', but in modern usage the hyphen is frequently omitted.

reciprocal pronoun is used to convey the idea of reciprocity or a two-way relationship. The **reciprocal pronouns** are 'each other' and 'one another'. Examples include 'They don't love each other any more', 'They seem to hate each other', 'We must try to help each other', 'The children were calling one another names', 'The two families were always criticizing one another' and 'The members of the family blame one another for their mother's death'.

reduplication refers to the process by which words are cre-

ated by repetition or by semi-repetition. These includ
'argy-bargy', 'dilly-dally', 'shilly-shally', 'flimflam
'heebie-jeebies', 'hocus-pocus', 'hugger-mugger
'knick-knack', and 'mish-mash'.

reflexive pronoun is one which refers back to a noun c
pronoun which has occurred earlier in the same sentenc
The **reflexive pronouns** include 'myself', 'ourselves'
'yourself', 'yourselves'; 'himself', 'herself', 'itself
'themselves'. Examples include 'The children washe
themselves', 'He cut himself shaving', 'Have you hu
yourself?' and 'She has cured herself of the habit'.

Reflexive pronouns are sometimes used for emphasi
as in 'The town itself was not very interesting' and 'Th
headmaster himself punished the boys'. They can also b
used to indicate that something has been done by some
body by his/her own efforts without any help, as in 'H
built the house himself', 'We converted the attic our
selves'. They can also indicate that someone or somethin
is alone, as in 'She lives by herself' and 'The house stand
by itself'.

regular verb see **irregular verb**.

relative clause is a subordinate clause which has the func
tion of an adjective. It is introduced by a **relative pro
noun.** *See* RELATIVE PRONOUNS.

relative pronouns introduce **relative clauses**. The **relativ
pronouns** are 'who', 'whom', 'whose', 'which' and
'that'. Examples of **relative clauses** introduced by rela
tive pronouns include 'There is the man who stole th
money', 'She is the person to whom I gave the money'
'This is the man whose wife won the prize', 'They criti

cized the work which he had done' and 'That's the house
that I would like to buy'. **Relative pronouns** refer back to
a noun or noun phrase in the main clause. These nouns
and noun phrases are known as 'antecedents'. The antecedents in the example sentences are respectively 'man',
'person', 'man', 'work' and 'house'.

Sometimes the **relative clause** divides the parts of the
main clause, as in 'The woman whose daughter is ill is
very upset', 'The people whom we met on holiday were
French' and 'The house that we liked best was too expensive'.

reported speech *see* **indirect speech**.

retro- is a prefix derived from Latin meaning 'back, backwards', as in 'retrograde', 'retrospect', 'retrorocket'.

retronym is a word or phrase that has had to be renamed
slightly in the light of another invention, etc. For example, an ordinary guitar has become 'acoustic guitar' because of the existence of 'electric guitar'. Leather has
sometimes become 'real leather' because of the existence
of 'imitation leather'.

rhetorical question is a question which is asked to achieve
some kind of effect and requires no answer. Examples include 'What's this country coming to?', 'Did you ever see
the like', 'Why do these things happen to me?', 'Where
did youth go?', 'Death, where is thy sting?' and 'Where
does time go?'.

root means the same as **base**.

S

second person refers to the person or thing to whom one i
talking. The term is applied to personal pronouns. The
second person singular whether acting as the subject of a
sentence is 'you', as in 'I told you so', 'We informed yo
of our decision' and 'They might have asked you sooner'
The **second person** personal pronoun does not alter it
form in the plural in English, unlike in some languages
The possessive form of the **second person** pronoun i
'yours' whether singular or plural, as in "He said to th
boys 'These books are not yours'"and 'This pen must b
yours'.

semi-colon is rather a rare and also rather formal form o
punctuation. It is mainly used between clauses that are no
joined by any form of conjunction, as in 'We had a won
derful holiday; sadly they did not', 'The children ar
tired; they are also hungry'. 'She was my sister; she wa
also my best friend' and 'He was a marvellous friend; h
is much missed'. A dash is sometimes used instead of
semi-colon but this more informal.

The **semi-colon** is also used to form subsets in a lon
list or series of names so that the said list seems less com
plex, as in 'The young man who wants to be a journalis
has applied everywhere. He has applied to *The Times* i

London; *The Washington Post* in Washington; *The Globe and Mail* in Toronto; *The Age* in Melbourne; *The Tribune* in Chicago.

The **semi-colon** is also sometimes used before 'however', 'nevertheless' 'hence', etc, as in 'He comes from Scotland; hence his nickname of Jock', 'We have extra seats for the concert; however you must not feel obliged to come'.

sentence is at the head of the hierarchy of grammar. All the other elements, such as words, phrases and clauses go to make up sentences. It is difficult to define a sentence. In terms of recognizing a sentence visually it can be described as beginning with a capital letter and ending with a full stop, or with an equivalent to the full stop, such as an exclamation mark. One suggested definition is that it is 'the complete expression of a single thought' but this seems rather a philosophical definition. Perhaps all one can say is that a sentence is a unit of grammar that can stand alone and make sense and obeys certain grammatical rules, such as usually having a subject and a predicate, as in 'The girl banged the door', where 'the girl' is the 'subject' and 'the door' is the predicate. *See* MAJOR SENTENCE, SIMPLE SENTENCE, COMPLEX SENTENCE.

simile is a figure of speech in which something is compared with another and said to be like it. This is in contradistinction to 'metaphor' where one thing is said actually to be another. Examples of similes include 'She is like an angel', 'Her hair is like silk', Her eyes are like forget-me-nots. 'The old man's skin is like leather', He swims like a fish'.

simple sentence is a sentence which cannot be broken

down into other causes. It generally contains a finite verb
Simple sentences include 'The man stole the car', 'She
nudged him' and 'He kicked the ball. See COMPLEX SEN-
TENCE and COMPOUND SENTENCE.

sexism was formerly widespread in the English language
whether this was intentional or not. Efforts are now being
made to rectify this situation, although some of the suggestions made are rather extreme. These suggestions include 'herstory' for 'history' and the replacement of man
by person ludicrous degree, as 'personhole' for 'man-
hole'. Most of these rather extreme ideas have not gained
widespread currency. Sensible progress has, however
been made. *See* HE; EACH; -MAN and -PERSON.

singular noun refers to 'one' rather than 'more than one'
which is the plural form. *See* PLURAL; IRREGULAR PLURAL.

spelling *see* **Appendix I**.

split infinitive refers to an infinitive which has had another
word in the form of an adverb, placed between itself and
'to', as in 'to rudely push' and 'to quietly leave'. This was
once considered a a great grammatical sin but the **split infinitive** is becoming acceptable in modern usage. In any
case it sometimes makes for a clumsy sentence if one
slavishly adheres to the correct form.

spoonerism refers to the accidental or deliberate transposi-
tion of the initial letters of two or more words, as in 'the
queer old dean' instead of 'the dear old queen', 'a blush-
ing crow' instead of a 'crushing blow' and 'a well-boiled
icicle' instead of a 'well-oiled bicycle'. **Spoonerism** is
called after the Reverend William Archibald Spooner
(1844–1930) of Oxford University.

ative present *see* **tense**.

rong verb is the more common term for 'irregular verb'. *See* IRREGULAR VERB.

bject of a sentence or clause is usually either a noun, as in 'Birds fly' (birds is the noun as subject); a noun phrase, as in 'The people in the town dislike him' (the people in the town' is the subject); a pronoun, as in 'She hit the child' (she is the pronoun as subject); a proper noun, as in 'Paris is the capital of France'. *See* DUMMY SUBJECT.

bjunctive *see* **mood**.

bordinate clause is dependent on another clause, namely he 'main' clause. Unlike the main clause, it cannot stand lone and make sense. **Subordinate clauses** are introduced by conjunctions. Examples of conjunctions which introduce subordinate clauses include 'after', 'before', when', 'if', 'because' and 'since'. *See* ADVERBIAL CLAUSE; NOUN CLAUSE.

ffix is an 'affix' which goes at the beginning of a word. Pre-' is a suffix in 'prepare' and 'pre-holiday'. *See* AFFIX.

perlative forms of of adjectives and adverbs follow the ame rules as comparative forms, except that they end in -*st* instead of -*er* and the longer ones use 'most' instead of more'.

llepsis is another word for **zeugma**.

necdoche is a figure of speech in which the part is put for he whole. For example 'The power of the Sceptre is fading' where sceptre is used for 'monarch'. 'The country as a fleet of a hundred sail' where 'sail' is used for ship'. 'He had a very successful career on the boards' where 'boards' is used for 'stage'.

T

tautology refers to unnecessary repetition, as in 'new inn⟨o⟩vations', 'a see-through transparent material' and 'one a⟨f⟩ter the other in succession'.

techno- is a prefix derived from Greek meaning 'craft, ski⟨ll⟩ as in 'technical', 'technology', 'technique' and 'technocra⟨t⟩

tele- is a prefix derived from Greek meaning 'distance' in 'telegraph', 'telephone', 'telescope' and 'television'.

tense is used to show the time at which the action of a ve⟨rb⟩ takes place. One of the tenses in English is the 'prese⟨nt⟩ tense'. It is used to indicate an action now going on or ⟨a⟩ state now existing. A distinction can be made between t⟨he⟩ 'habitual present', which marks habitual or repeated a⟨c⟩tions or recurring events, and the 'stative present', whi⟨ch⟩ indicates something that is true at all times. Examples ⟨of⟩ 'habitual present' include 'He works long hours' and 'S⟨he⟩ walks to work'. Examples of the 'stative tense' inclu⟨de⟩ 'The world is round' and 'Everyone must die eventuall⟨y⟩

The 'progressive present' or 'continuous present' ⟨is⟩ formed with the verb 'to be' and the 'present participl⟨e⟩ as in ,He is walking to the next village', 'They are thi⟨nk⟩ing about leaving' ,'She was driving along the road wh⟨en⟩ she saw him' and 'They were worrying about the state ⟨of⟩ the economy'

The 'past tense' refers to an action or state which has taken place before the present time. In the case of 'irregular verbs' it is formed by adding *-ed* to the base form of the verb, as in 'fear/feared', 'look/looked', and 'turn/turned'. For the past tense of 'irregular verbs', *see* IRREGULAR VERBS.

The 'future tense' refers to an action or state that will take place at some time in the future. It is formed with 'will' and 'shall'. Traditionally 'will' was used with the second and third person pronouns ('you', 'he/she/it', 'they') and 'shall' with the first person ('I' and 'we'), as in 'You will be bored', 'He will soon be home', 'They will leave tomorrow', 'I shall buy some bread' and 'We shall go by train'. Also traditionally 'shall was used with the second and third persons to indicate emphasis , insistence, determination, refusal, etc., as in 'You shall go to the ball' and 'He shall not be admitted'. 'Will' was used with the first person in the same way, as in 'I will get even with him' and 'We will get our money back'.

In modern usage 'will' is generally used for the first person as well as for second and third, as in 'I will see you tomorrow' and 'We will be there soon' and 'shall' is used for emphasis, insistence, etc. for first, second and third persons.

The 'future tense' can also be formed with the use of 'be about to' or 'be going to', as in 'We were about to leave' and 'They were going to look for somewhere to live'.

Other tenses include the 'perfect tense' which is formed using the verb 'to have' and the past participle. In the case of 'regular verbs' the 'past participle' is formed by adding 'ed' to the base form of the verb. For the past particip[l] of 'irregular verbs' see irregular verbs. Examples of t[h] 'perfect tense' include 'He has played his last match','W[e] have travelled all day' and 'They have thought a lot ab[out] it'.

The 'past perfect tense' or 'pluperfect tense' is form[ed] using the verb 'to have' and the past participle, as in 'S[he] had no idea that he was dead', 'We had worked as hard [as] possible' and 'They had felt unhappy about the situatio[n]

The 'future perfect' is formed using the verb 'to hav[e] and the pas participle,as in 'He will have arrived by no[w] and 'W[e] will have been away for four years by then.'

the usually refers back to something already identified or something specific, as in 'Where is the key?, 'What ha[ve] you done with the book which I gave you?' and 'We ha[ve] found the book which we lost'. It is also used to den[ote] someone or something as being the only one, as in 't[he] House of Lords', 'the King of Spain' and 'the President [of] Russia' and to indicate a class or group, as in 'the arist[oc] racy', the cat family' and 'the teaching profession'. The [is] sometimes pronounced 'thee' when it is used to identi[fy] someone or something unique or important, as in 'Is th[at] the John Frame over there?' and She is the fashion d[e] signer of the moment'.

they see he.

third person refers to a third party not the speaker or t[he] person or thing being spoken to. Note that 'person' in t[his] context can refer to things as well as people. 'Person' [in] this sense applies to personal pronouns. The third pers[on] singular forms are 'he', 'she' and 'it' when the subject a sentence or clause, as in 'She will win' and 'It will be fine'. The third person singular forms are 'him', 'her','it' when the object, as in 'His behaviour hurt her' and 'She meant it'. The third person plural is 'they' when the subject, as in 'They have left' and 'They were angry' and 'them' when the object, as in 'His words made them angry' and 'We accompanied them.

The possessive forms of the singular are 'his', 'hers' and 'its', as in 'he played his guitar' and 'The dog hurt its leg' and the the possessive form of the plural is theirs,as in 'That car is theirs' and 'They say that the book is theirs'. See he.

to-infinitive refers to the 'infinitive' form of the verb when it is accompanied by 'to' rather than when it is the 'bare infinitive' without 'to'. Examples of the **to-infinitive** include 'We were told to go' ,'I didn't want to stay' and 'To get there on time we'll have to leave now'.

transitive verb is a verb which takes a 'direct object'. In the sentence 'The boy broke the window' 'window' is a 'direct object' and so 'broke' (breakO is a transitive verb. In the sentence 'She eats fruit' 'fruit' is a 'direct object' and so 'eat' is a transitive verb. In the sentence 'They kill enemy soldiers' 'enemy soldiers' is a 'direct object' and so 'kill' is a transitive verb'. See direct object and intransitive verb.

trisyllabic means having three syllables. Examples include 'monument', 'relative' and 'satisfy'.

U

ultra- is a prefix derived from Latin meaning 'beyond', in 'ultraviolet' and 'ltramodern'.

umlaut refers to the diacritic which indicates a change vowel sound in German, as in *mädchen*.

un- is a prefix with two meanings. It can mean either 'no as in 'unclean', 'untrue' and 'unwise'. it can also me: 'back, reversal', as in 'undo', 'unfasten', 'unlatch' a 'untie'.

uncount noun see uncountable noun.

uncountable noun refers to a noun that is not usual pluralized or 'counted'. Such a noun is usually preced by 'some', rather than 'a'. **Uncountable nouns** often r fer to substances or commodities or qualities, process and states. Examples of uncountable nouns include butte china, luggage, petrol, sugar, heat, information, povert richness and warmth.In some situations it is possible have a countable version of what is usually an **uncoun able noun.** Thus 'sugar' is usually considered to be : 'uncountable noun' but it can be used in a 'countabl form in contexts such as 'I take two sugars in my coff please'. Some nouns exist in an uncountable and 'coun able' form. Examples include 'cake', as in 'Have son cake' and 'She ate three cakes' and 'She could not paint for lack of light' and 'the lights went out'.

uni- is a prefix derived from Latin meaning 'one' , as in unicycle, unilateral and unity.

V

verb is often known as a 'doing' word. Although this rather restrictive ,since it tends to preclude auxilia verbs, modal verbs, etc. the verb is the word in a senten that is most concerned with the action and is usually e sential to the structure of the sentence. **Verbs** 'inflect' ar indicate tense, voice, mood, number, number and perso Most of the information on **Verbs** has been placed und related entries. See active, passive, voice, auxiliary ver modal verb, mood, finite verb, non-finite verb, transiti verb, intransitive verb, irregular verb, linking verb, -i forms and phrasal verbs.

verb phrase refers to a group of verb forms which has t same function as a single verb. Examples include 'ha been raining', 'must have been lying', should not ha been doing and 'has been seen doing'.

virgule is a rare word for oblique.

vocative case is relevant mainly to languages suchas Lat which are based on cases and inflections. In English t vocative is expressed by addressing someons, as 'Joh could I se you for a minute' or by some form of greetin endearment or exclamation.

voice is one of the categories that describes verbs. It i volves two different ways of looking at the action of verbs. It is divided into 'active voice' and 'passive voice'. See active and passive.

W

weak verb is a less common term for 'regular verb'. See irregular verb.

who and **whom** take information from Usage Guide See relative clause.

whose and **whose** are liable to be confused because they sound the same. However they are not at all the same. Who's is a contraction of 'who is' and is used in speech and informal written contexts, as in 'Who's going to the cinema?', 'Who's been eating garlic?' and 'Who's afraid of spiders'. **Whose** is a possessive pronoun or possessive adjective, as in 'That's the woman whose house was burgled', 'Whose hat is this?' and 'Whose are they?'.

-ways is prefix which to some extent acts an alternative to 'wise' in its first two meanings, as in crabways and lengthways.

-wise is a prefix with several meanings. It can mean 'indicating manner or way', as in clockwise and crabwise. It can also mean' in the position or direction of' as in lengthwise and breadthwise. It can also mean 'with reference to', as in 'careerwise, familywise. jobwise and salarywise. This last use is very much over-used. -Wise can also mean 'clever, sensible', as in streetwise and worldlywise.

Z

zero plural refers to a plural form that has the same form as the singular. Examples include 'cod', 'deer', 'grouse' (gamebird) and 'sheep'. Some nouns have ordinary plurals and **zero plurals** as alternatives, as 'fish/fishes'. Nouns of measurement often have **zero plurals** , as in 'She is five foot three' and 'Six dozen eggs'.

zeugma is a figure of speech which uses a single word to apply to two words which are not appropriate to each other , as in 'We collected our coats and our baby', 'She left the building and her job' and 'She left in taxi and a fit of hysterics'. **Zeugma** is similar to bathos.

Appendix I

Some words with totally different meanings have similar spellings and therefore can be easily confused.
Some examples are:

aboard	affect	allusion	angel
abroad	effect	delusion	angle
		illusion	
accept	affluent		annals
except	effluent	altar	annuals
		alter	
access	ail		annex
excess	ale	alteration	annexe
		altercation	
acme	air		annuals
acne	heir	alternately	annals
		alternatively	
ad	all		antiquated
add	awl	amateur	antique
		amateurish	
adapter	allay		arc
adaptor	alley	amend	ark
		emend	
addition	allegory		arisen
dition	allergy	amiable	arose
		amicable	
adverse	alley		artist
averse	allay	among	artiste
		between	
advice	alliterate		ascent
advise	illiterate	amoral	assent
		immoral	
aesthetic	allude	immortal	ascetic
ascetic	elude		aesthetic

assay	ball	bean	belief
essay	bawl	been	believe
		being	
assent	ballet		bell
ascent	ballot	beat	belle
		beet	
astrology	banns		bellow
astronomy	bans	beau	below
		bow	
ate	bare		beret
eaten	bear	became	berry
		become	bury
aural	barn		
oral	baron	beech	berth
	barren	beach	birth
averse			
adverse	base	been	beside
	bass	bean	besides
awl		being	
all	bated		between
	baited	beer	among
axes		bier	
axis	bath		bid
	bathe	beet	bade
bad		beat	
bade	baton		bier
	batten	befallen	beer
bade		befell	
bid	bawl		bight
	ball	began	bite
bail		begun	
bale	bazaar		birth
bale out	bizarre	being	berth
		bean	
baited	beach	been	bit
bated	beech		bitten

ite	bookie	bow	breech
ight	bouquet	bough	breach
izarre	boor	boy	bridal
azaar	boar	buoy	bridle
	bore		
lew		brae	broach
lown	boost	bray	brooch
	boast		
lew		brake	broke
lue	bootee	break	broken
	booty		
loc		brassière	brooch
lock	bore	brazier	broach
	boar		
lond	boor	bray	buffet
londe		brae	[buffit]
	bore		buffet
lown	born	brazier	[boofa]
lew	borne	brassière	
			buoy
lue	borough	breach	boy
lew	burgh	breech	
			burgh
oar	bough	bread	borough
oor	bow	bred	
ore			bury
	bound	break	beret
oard	bounded	brake	berry
ored			
	bouquet	breath	but
oast	bookie	breathe	butt
oost			
	blow	bred	buy
onny	beau	bread	by
ony			bye

cache	cartilage	cereal	chord
cash	cartridge	serial	cord
caddie	carton	chafe	chose
caddy	cartoon	chaff	choose
			chosen
calf	cartridge	charted	
calve	cartilage	chartered	chute
			shoot
callous	cash	chased	
callus	cache	chaste	cite
			sight
calve	cast	cheap	site
calf	caste	cheep	
			clothes
came	cavalier	check	cloths
come	cavalry	cheque	
			coarse
canned	ceiling	checked	course
could	sealing	chequered	
			collage
cannon	cell	cheep	college
canon	sell	cheap	
			coma
can't	cellular	cheque	comma
cant	cellulose	check	
			come
canvas	censor	chilli	came
canvass	censure	chilly	
			comma
carat	cent	choir	coma
carrot	scent	quire	
	sent		commission-
cart		choose	aire
kart	centenarian	chose	commissioner
	centenary	chosen	

complement · cord · council · cygnet
compliment · chord · counsel · signet
· · consul ·
· · · cymbal
complemen- · co-respond- · · symbol
tary · ent · councillor ·
complimen- · correspond- · counsellor ·
tary · ent · · diary
· · coup · diary
concert · cornet · coop ·
consort · coronet · · dam
· · course · damn
confidant · cornflour · coarse ·
confidante · cornflower · · dammed
confident · · courtesy · damned
· coronet · curtsy ·
conscience · cornet · · damn
conscientious · · creak · dam
conscious · corps · creek ·
· corpse · · dear
consort · · crevasse · deer
concert · corral · crevice ·
· coral · · decry
consul · · crochet · descry
council · correspond- · crotchet ·
counsel · ent · · deer
· co-respond- · cue · dear
continual · ent · queue ·
continuous · · · delusion
· cost · curb · allusion
coop · costed · kerb · illusion
coup · · ·
· could · currant · dependant
coral · canned · current · dependent
corral · · ·
· · curtsy · deprecate
· · courtesy · depreciate

descendant	discus	drunk	earthly
descendent	discuss	drank	earthy
descry	doe	dual	easterly
decry	dough	duel	eastern
desert	doily	ducks	eaten
dessert	dolly	dux	ate
			eclipse
device	done	dudgeon	ellipse
devise	did	dungeon	
			economic
devolution	dough	due	economical
evolution	doe	dew	
		Jew	edition
dew	draft		addition
due	draught	duel	
Jew		dual	eerie
	dragon		eyrie
diary	dragoon	dully	
dairy		duly	effect
	draught		affect
did	draft	dungeon	
done		dudgeon	effluent
	drawn		affluent
die	drew	dux	
dye		ducks	elder
	drank		eldest
died	drunk	dye	
dyed		die	elicit
	drew		illicit
dinghy	drawn	dyed	
dingy		died	eligible
	driven		legible
disbelief	drove	dyeing	
disbelieve		dying	

ellipse
eclipse

elude
allude

emend
amend

emigrant
immigrant

emigration
immigration

emission
omission

emphasis
emphasize

employee
employer

ensure
insure

entomologist
etymologist

envelop
envelope

epigram
epitaph
epithet

ere
err

erotic
erratic

err
ere

erratic
erotic

escapement
escarpment

essay
assay

etymologist
entomologist

evolution
devolution

ewe
yew
you

except
accept

excess
access

executioner
executor

exercise
exorcise

expand
expend

expansive
expensive

expatiate
expiate

expend
expand

expensive
expansive

expiate
expatiate

extant
extinct

eyrie
eerie

faerie
fairy

fain
feign

faint
feint

fair
fare

fairy
faerie

fallen
fell
felled

fare
fair

fate
fête

faun
fawn

feat
feet

feign
fain

feint
faint

fell
fallen
felled

ferment
foment

fête	flocks	fore	forty
fate	phlox	four	fort
			forte
fiancé	floe	foregone	
fiancée	flow	forgone	forward
			foreword
filed	flour	foresaw	
filled	flower	foreseen	forwent
			forgone
final	floury	foreword	
finale	flowery	forward	foul
			fowl
fir	flow	forgave	
fur	flow	forgiven	found
			founded
fission	flower	forgone	
fissure	flour	foregone	fount
			font
flair	flowery	forgone	
flare	floury	forwent	four
			fore
flammable	flown	forgot	
inflammable	flew	forgotten	fourth
			forth
flare	flue	forsaken	
flair	flue	forsook	fowl
	flew		foul
flea		forswore	
flee		forsworn	franc
	foment		frank
	ferment	fort	
flew		forte	freeze
flu	font	forty	frieze
flue	fount		
		forth	froze
flew	forbade	fourth	frozen
flown	forbidden		

funeral | genteel | grate | hail
funereal | gentile | great | hale
| gentle | |
fur | | grew | hair
fir | genus | grown | hare
| genie | |
gabble | genius | grief | half
gable | | grieve | halve
| gild | |
gaff | guild | grill | hallo
gaffe | | grille | hallow
| gilt | | halo
gait | guilt | griped |
gate | | gripped | halve
| given | | half
galleon | gave | grisly |
gallon | | gristly | hangar
| glacier | grizzly | hanger
gamble | glazier | |
gambol | | grope | hanged
| goal | group | hung
gaol | gaol | |
goal | | ground | hanger
| gone | grounded | hangar
gate | went | |
gait | | grown | hare
| gorilla | grew | hair
gave | guerrilla | |
given | | guerrilla | hart
| gourmand | gorilla | heart
genie | gourmet | |
genius | | guild | heal
genus | gradation | gild | heel
| graduation | |
| | guilt | hear
| | gilt | here

heart	hoard	hymn	impracticable
hart	horde	him	impractical
heel	hoarse	idle	inapt
heal	horse	idol	inept
heir	hole	illegible	incredible
air	whole	ineligible	incredulous
here	honorary	illicit	indigenous
hear	honourable	elicit	indigent
heron	hoop	illiterate	industrial
herring	whoop	alliterate	industrious
hew	hoped	illusion	ineligible
hue	hopped	allusion	illegible
		delusion	
hewed	horde		inept
hewn	hoard	immigrant	inapt
		emigrant	
hid	horse		inflammable
hidden	hoarse	immigration	flammable
		emigration	
higher	hue		ingenious
hire	hew	immoral	ingenuous
		amoral	
him	human	immortal	inhuman
hymn	humane		inhumane
		immorality	
hire	humiliation	immortality	insure
higher	humility		ensure
		impetuous	
hoar	hung	impetus	intelligent
whore	hanged		intelligible

interment	knead	lain	leak
internment	kneed	lane	leek
	need		
invertebrate		lair	led
inveterate	knew	layer	lead
	known		
jam		lama	lee
jamb	knew	llama	lea
	new		
Jew		lane	leek
dew	knight	lain	leak
due	night		
		laterally	legible
jib	knightly	latterly	eligible
jibe	nightly		
		lath	lemming
judicial	knit	lathe	lemon
judicious	nit		
		latterly	leopard
junction	knot	laterally	leper
juncture	not		
		lay	lessen
kart	knotty	lade	lesson
cart	naughty	laid	
		lied	liable
kerb	know		libel
curb	no	layer	
		lair	liar
key	known		lyre
quay	knew	lea	
		lee	libel
knave	lade		liable
nave	laid	lead	
	lay	led	licence
	lied		license

lied	lone	made	marshal
lade	loan	maid	martial
laid			
lay	looped	magnate	marten
	loped	magnet	martin
lightening	lopped		
lightning		maid	martial
	loose	made	marshal
lineament	lose		
liniment		mail	martin
	loot	male	marten
liqueur	lute		
liquor		main	mask
	loped	mane	masque
literal	lopped		
literary	looped	maize	mat
literate		maze	matt
	lose		
llama	loose	male	mayor
lama		mail	mare
	loth		
load	loathe	mane	maze
lode		main	maize
	lumbar		
loan	lumber	maniac	mean
lone		manic	mien
	lute		
loath	loot	manner	meat
loathe		manor	meet
	lyre		mete out
local	liar	mare	
locale		mayor	medal
			meddle
	macaroni	marina	
lode	macaroon	merino	
load			mediate
			meditate

⌐eet	missal	motif	navel
⌐eat	missile	motive	naval
⌐ete out			
	mistaken	mouse	navvy
⌐erino	mistook	moose	navy
⌐arina		mousse	
	mite		nay
⌐etal	might	mucous	née
⌐ettle		mucus	neigh
	moat		
⌐ete out	mote	multiple	need
⌐eat		multiply	knead
⌐eet	modal		kneed
	model	muscle	
⌐eter	module	mussel	negligent
⌐etre			negligible
	momentary	muse	
⌐ettle	momentous	mews	neigh
⌐etal	momentum		nay
		mussel	née
⌐ews	moose	muscle	
⌐use	mouse		net
	mousse	mystic	nett
⌐ien		mystique	
⌐ean	moped		new
	mopped	naught	knew
⌐ight		nought	
⌐ite	moral		night
	morale	naughty	knight
⌐iner		knotty	
⌐inor	morality		nightly
	mortality	naval	knightly
⌐inister		navel	
⌐inster	mote		nit
	moat	nave	knit
		knave	

no	organism	palate	peak
know	orgasm	palette	peek
		pallet	pique
northerly	outdid		
northern	outdone	pale	peal
		pail	peel
not	overcame		
knot	overcome	palette	pear
		palate	pair
nougat	overdid	pallet	pare
nugget	overdone		
		pane	pearl
nought	overran	pain	purl
naught	overrun		
		par	peasant
nugget	overtaken	parr	pheasant
nougat	overtook		
		pare	pedal
oar	overthrew	pear	peddle
ore	overthrown	pair	
			peek
of	packed	parr	peak
off	pact	par	pique
official	pail	passed	peel
officious	pale	past	peal
omission	pain	pastel	peer
emission	pane	pastille	pier
oral	pair	pate	pence
aural	pare	pâté	pennies
	pear	patty	
ore			pendant
oar		peace	pendent
		piece	

ennies	pistil	pore	price
ence	pistol	pour	prise
			prize
erquisite	pizza	pored	
erequisite	piazza	poured	principal
			principle
ersonal	place	poser	
ersonnel	plaice	poseur	prise
			price
etrel	plain	pour	prize
etrol	plane	pore	
			private
heasant	plaintiff	poured	privet
easant	plaintive	pored	
			prize
hlox	plait	practicable	prise
ocks	plate	practical	price
iazza	plane	practice	proceed
izza	plain	practise	precede
iece	plate	pray	profit
eace	plait	prey	prophet
ier	plum	precede	program
eer	plumb	proceed	programme
ined	politic	premier	proof
inned	political	première	prove
iped	pool	prerequisite	property
ipped	pull	perquisite	propriety
ique	poplar	prey	prophecy
eak	popular	pray	prophesy
eek			

prophet	quite	raped	reign
profit	quiet	rapped	rain
			rein
propriety	racket	rapped	
property	racquet	rapt	relief
		wrapped	relieve
prostate	radar		
prostate	raider	rated	reproof
		ratted	reprove
prove	raged		
proof	ragged	raze	respectful
		raise	respective
pull	raider		
pool	radar	read	rest
		red	wrest
purl	rain		
pearl	reign	read	retch
	rein	reed	wretch
put			
putt	raise	real	review
	raze	reel	revue
quash			
squash	rampant	red	rhyme
	rampart	read	rime
quay			
key	ran	reel	ridden
	run	real	rode
queue			
cue	rang	refuge	right
	ringed	refugee	rite
quiet	rung		write
quite		regal	
	rap	regale	rime
quire	wrap		rhyme
choir			

ng	rout	saviour	sear
ring	route	savour	seer
			sere
aged	row	saw	
ng	roe	seen	secret
ng			secrete
	rowed	sawed	
en	road	sawn	see
se	rode		sea
		scared	
e	ruff	scarred	seem
ght	rough		seam
rite		scene	
	run	seen	seen
ad	ran		saw
de		scent	
wed	rung	cent	seen
	wrung	sent	scene
de			
lden	rye	sceptic	seer
	wry	septic	sear
			sere
e	sail	scraped	
w	sale	scrapped	sell
			cell
le	salon	sculptor	
l	saloon	sculpture	sensual
			sensuous
se		sea	
en	sang	see	sent
	sung		scent
te		sealing	scent
rote	sank	ceiling	
	sunk		
ugh	sunken		septic
ff			sceptic
		seam	
		seem	

sere	sheared	singeing	sniped
sear	sheered	singing	snipped
seer	shorn		
		sinuous	so
serial	shelf	sinus	sew
cereal	shelve		sow
		site	
series	shoe	cite	soar
serious	shoo	sight	sore
sew	shook	skies	sociable
so	shaken	skis	social
sow			
	shoot	slain	solder
sewed	chute	slew	soldier
sewn			
	shorn	slated	sole
sewer	sheared	slatted	soul
sower	sheered		
		slay	some
sewn	showed	sleigh	sum
sewed	shown		
		slew	son
sewn	shrank	slain	sun
sown	shrunk		
		sloe	soot
sextant	sight	slow	suit
sexton	cite		
	site	sloped	sore
shaken		slopped	soar
shook	signet		
	cygnet	slow	soul
shear		sloe	sole
sheer	silicon		
	silicone	smelled	southerly
		smelt	southern

ow	stair	steal	striped
ew	stare	steel	stripped
o			
	stake	step	strive
owed	steak	steppe	strife
own			
	stalk	stile	striven
ower	stock	style	strove
ewer			
	stanch	stimulant	stunk
own	staunch	stimulus	stank
ewn			
	stank	stock	sty
pared	stunk	stalk	stye
parred			
	stare	stocked	style
peciality	stair	stoked	stile
pecialty			
	stared	storey	suede
pecies	starred	story	swede
pecious			
	stationary	straight	suit
ped	stationery	strait	soot
peeded			
	statue	straightened	suite
poke	statute	straitened	sweet
poken			
	staunch	stratum	sum
prang	stanch	stratus	some
prung			
	stayed	strewed	summary
quash	staid	strewn	summery
uash			
	steak	strife	sun
taid	stake	strive	son
ayed			

sundae	swum	tea	thorough
Sunday	swam	tee	through
sung	symbol	team	thrash
sang	cymbal	teem	thresh
sunk	tacks	tear	threw
sank	tax	tare	through
sunken			
	tail	tear	threw
super	tale	tier	thrown
supper			
	taken	tee	throes
surplice	took	tea	throws
surplus			
	tale	teem	throne
swam	tail	team	thrown
swum			
	taped	teeth	through
swede	tapped	teethe	thorough
suede			
	taper	temporal	through
sweet	tapir	temporary	threw
suite			
	tapped	tendon	thrown
swelled	taped	tenon	throne
swollen			
	tare	tenor	throws
swingeing	tear	tenure	throes
swinging			
	taught	testimonial	thyme
swollen	taut	testimony	time
swelled			
	tax	their	tic
swore	tacks	there	tick
sworn		they're	

tier	topi	tyre	vertex
tear	toupee	tire	vortex
tiled	tore	unaware	vigilant
tilled	torn	unawares	vigilante
timber	tow	unconscion-	vocation
timbre	toe	able	vacation
		unconscious	
time	trait		voracity
thyme	tray	undid	veracity
		undone	
tire	treaties		vortex
tyre	treatise	unwanted	vertex
		unwonted	
to	trod		wafer
too	trodden	urban	waver
two		urbane	
	troop		waged
toe	troupe		wagged
tow		vacation	
	tun	vocation	waif
tomb	ton		waive
tome	tonne		wave
		vain	
ton	turban	vane	waist
tonne	turbine	vein	waste
tun			
	two	vale	want
too	to	veil	wont
to	too		
two		venal	warden
	tycoon	venial	warder
took	typhoon		
taken		veracity	ware
		voracity	wear

waste	whole	wore	write
waist	hole	worn	right
			rite
wave	whoop	would	
waif	hoop	willed	wrote
waive			rote
	whore	would	
waver	hoar	wood	wrote
wafer		wooed	written
	willed		
way	would	wove	wrung
weigh		woven	rung
	winded		
weak	wound	wrap	wry
week		rap	rye
	wit		
wear	whit	wrapped	yew
ware		rapped	ewe
	withdrawn	rapt	you
weekly	withdrew		
weakly		wreak	yoke
	wittily	wreck	yolk
weigh	wittingly		
way		wreath	yore
	woe	wreathe	your
went	woo		
gone		wrest	
	woke	rest	
westerly	woken		
western		wretch	
	wont	retch	
wet	want		
whet		wring	
	woo	ring	
whit	woe		
wit			

Appendix II

All of us have problem words that cause spelling difficulties but there are some words that are generally misspelt. These include:

A

abbreviation	acquit	afforestation
abscess	acquittal	aggravate
absence	acreage	aggravation
abysmal	across	aggregate
accelerator	actual	aggression
accessible	additional	aggressive
accessories	address	aghast
accommodate	adequate	agnosticism
accompaniment	adieu	agoraphobia
accumulate	adjacent	agreeable
accurate	admissible	agreed
accustomed	admittance	aisle
achieve	adolescence	alcohol
aching	adolescent	alfresco
acknowledge	advantageous	alibis
acknowledgement/	advertisement	align
acknowledgment	advice	alignment
acquaint	advise	allege
acquaintance	aerate	allergic
acquiesce	aerial	alleys
acquiescence	aesthetic	alligator
acquire	affect	allocate
	affiliation	allotment

allotted	anorak	ascent
almond	answered	asphalt
alms	Antarctic	asphyxiate
alphabetically	antibiotic	asphyxiation
already	antithesis	assassin
although	anxiety	assassinate
aluminium	apartheid	assessment
ambiguous	apologize	assistance
amethyst	appalling	associate
ammunition	apparently	asthma
anachronism	appearance	asthmatic
anaesthetic	appendicitis	astrakhan
analyse	appreciate	atheist
analysis	approval	atrocious
anarchist	aquarium	attach
ancestor	aquiline	attendant
ancestry	arbiter	attitude
anemone	arbitrary	aubergine
angrily	arbitration	auburn
anguish	archaeology	auctioneer
annihilate	architectural	audible
annihilation	Arctic	aural
anniversary	arguably	automatic
announcement	arrangement	autumn
annulled	arrival	awful
annulment	artichoke	awkward
anonymous	ascend	

B

bachelor
bagatelle
baggage
bailiff
ballast
ballerina
banana
banister
bankruptcy
banquet
barbecue
barometer
barrister
basically
basis
bassoon
battalion
bazaar
beautiful
befriend
beguile
behaviour
beleaguer
belief
believe
belligerent

benefited
bequeath
berserk
besiege
bettered
bevelled
bewitch
bias
bicycle
biennial
bigamous
bigoted
bilingual
biscuit
bivouacked
blancmange
blasphemous
blasphemy
bleary
blitz
bodily
bonfire
bootee
borough
bouquet
bourgeois
boutique

bracketed
braille
brassiere
breadth
breathalyser
brief
broccoli
brochure
bronchitis
bruise
brusque
buccaneer
Buddhist
budding
budgerigar
budgeted
buffeted
bulletin
bumptious
bungalow
buoyancy
buoyant
bureau
bureaucracy
business
buttoned

C

cabbage
cafeteria
caffeine
camouflage
campaign
campaigned
cancelled
cancerous
candour
cannabis
cannibal
canvassing
capability
capillary
capitalist
caravan
carbohydrate
carburettor
career
caress
caries
carriage
cartoonist
cashier
cassette
castanets

casualty
catalogue
catarrh
catechism
catering
cauliflower
cautious
ceiling
cellophane
cemetery
centenary
centilitre
centimetre
certainty
champagne
championed
chancellor
changeable
channelled
characteristic
chasm
chauffeur
cheetah
cherish
chief
chilblain
chintz

chiropody
chisel
choreographer
choreography
chronically
chrysanthemum
cigarette
cinnamon
circuitous
cistern
civilian
claustrophobia
clientele
clique
coalesce
cocoa
coconut
coffee
cognac
coincidence
colander
collaborate
collapsible
colleague
colonel
colossal
comically

commandeer
commemorate
commentator
commercial
commiserate
commission
commissionaire
commitment
committal
committed
committee
communicate
commuter
companion
comparative
comparison
compatibility
compelled
competitive
computer
conceal
concealment
conceit
conceive
concession
concurrent
concussion

condemned
condescend
confectionery
conference
confetti
congeal
congratulations
conjunctivitis
conned
connoisseur
conscience
conscientious
conscious
consequently
consignment
consolation
conspicuous
constitute
consumer
contemptible
continent
continuous
contraception
contradictory
controlled
controller
controversial

convalesce
convenient
convertible
conveyed
convolvulus
coolly
cooperate
cooperative
coordinate
copying
coquette
corduroy
co-respondent
coronary
correspondence
correspondent
corridor
corroborate
corrugated
cosmopolitan
cosseted
councillor
counselling
counterfeit
courageous
courteous
crèche

credible	**D**	deliberate
credited	dachshund	delicatessen
crematorium	daffodil	delicious
creosote	dahlia	delinquent
crescent	dais	delirious
crisis	damage	demeanour
criterion	dandruff	demonstrate
crocheted	darkened	denouement
crocodile	debatable	denunciation
croupier	debauched	dependence
crucial	debility	depth
crucifixion	deceased	derailment
cruelly	deceit	dermatitis
cruise	deceive	derogatory
cryptic	deciduous	descend
cubicle	decipher	descendant
cupful	decoyed	desiccate
curable	decrease	desperate
curiosity	decreed	detach
curious	defamatory	detachable
currency	defeat	detergent
curriculum vitae	defendant	deterred
customary	defied	deterrent
cynic	definite	deuce
cynicism	definitely	develop
cynosure	dehydrate	developed
	deign	development

diabetes	discipline	dissipation
diagnosis	discotheque	dissociate
dialogue	discouraging	dissolute
diametrically	discourteous	dissuade
diaphragm	discrepancy	distilled
diarrhoea	discrimination	distillery
difference	discussion	distinguish
different	disease	distraught
dilapidated	disguise	disuse
dilemma	dishevelled	divisible
dilettante	dishonourable	documentary
diminish	disillusion	doggerel
diminution	disinfectant	domineering
dinosaur	disinherited	donate
diphtheria	dismissal	doubt
diphthong	disobeyed	dragooned
disadvantageous	disparage	drastically
disagreeable	dispelled	draughty
disagreed	disposal	drooled
disagreement	dispossess	drooped
disappearance	dissatisfaction	drunkenness
disappeared	dissatisfy	dubious
disappoint	dissect	dumbfounded
disapproval	disseminate	dungarees
disastrous	dissent	duress
disbelief	dissimilar	dutiful
disbelieve	dissipated	dynamite

dysentery
dyspepsia

E

eccentric
ecclesiastic
ecologically
economically
ecstasy
eczema
effective
effervescence
efficacious
efficient
effrontery
eightieth
elaborate
electrician
elevenses
eligible
emancipate
embarrass
embarrassment
emergence
emergent
emolument
emotional

emphasize
employee
emptied
enable
encourage
encyclopedia
endeavour
endurance
energetically
enervate
engineer
enough
ensuing
entailed
enthusiasm
enumerate
epilepsy
equalize
equalled
equipped
erroneous
erudite
escalator
escapism
espionage
essence
essential

estranged
etiquette
euthanasia
eventually
evidently
exaggerate
exaggeration
exalt
exasperate
exceed
exceedingly
excellent
excessive
exchequer
excommunicate
exercise
exhaust
exhibit
exhilarate
exorcise
explanation
exquisite
extinguish
extraneous
extravagant

F

fabulous
facetious
faeces
Fahrenheit
fallacious
fanatic
farcical
fascinate
fatigue
fatuous
February
feeler
feign
ferocious
festooned
feud
feudal
fevered
fiasco
fibre
fictitious
fiend
fierce
fiery
filial
finesse

flabbergasted
flaccid
flammable
flannelette
fluent
fluoridate
fluoride
fluoridize
foliage
forcible
foreigner
forfeit
forthwith
fortieth
fortuitous
fortunately
frailty
frankincense
fraudulent
freedom
freight
frequency
friend
frolicked
fuchsia
fugitive
fulfil

fulfilled
fulfilment
fullness
fulsome
furious
furniture
furthered

G

gaiety
galloped
garrison
garrotted
gases
gateau
gauge
gazetteer
geisha
generator
genuine
gerbil
gesticulate
ghastly
ghetto
gigantic
gingham
giraffe

glamorous
glamour
glimpse
global
gluttonous
glycerine
gnarled
gnash
goitre
gossiped
government
graffiti
grammar
grandeur
gratefully
gratitude
gratuitous
greetings
gregarious
grief
grieve
grovelled
gruesome
guarantee
guarantor
guard
guardian

guest
guillotine
guinea
guise
guitar
gymkhana
gypsy/gipsy

H

haemoglobin
haemorrhage
halcyon
hallucination
hammered
handfuls
handicapped
handkerchief
happened
harangue
harass
harlequin
haughty
hazard
hearse
height
heightened
heinous

heir
herbaceous
hereditary
heroism
hesitate
hiccup, hiccough
hideous
hierarchy
hieroglyphics
hijack
hilarious
hindrance
hippopotamus
holiday
holocaust
homonym
honorary
honour
hooligan
horoscope
horrible
horticulture
hullabaloo
humorous
humour
hurricane
hurried

hygiene
hyphen
hypnosis
hypochondria
hypocrisy
hypotenuse
hypothesis
hypothetical
hysterical

I

icicle
ideological
idiosyncrasy
ignorance
illegible
illegitimate
illiberal
illiterate
imaginative
imitation
immaculate
immediate
immemorial
immoral
immovable
impasse

impeccable
imperative
imperceptible
imperious
impetuous
implacable
impresario
imprisoned
imprisonment
inaccessible
inadmissible
inappropriate
inaugural
incandescent
incessant
incipient
incognito
incommunicado
inconceivable
incongruous
incontrovertible
incorrigible
incredulous
incriminate
incubator
incurred
indefatigable

indefinable
indefinite
independence
independent
indescribable
indict
indictment
indigenous
indigestible
indomitable
indubitable
ineligible
inescapable
inexcusable
inexhaustible
infallible
infatuated
inferred
infinitive
inflamed
inflammable
inflationary
ingratiate
ingredient
inhabitant
inheritance
inhibition

iniquitous
initiate
initiative
innate
innocuous
innumerable
innumerate
inoculate
insecticide
inseparable
insincere
insistence
instalment
instantaneous
intercept
interference
interior
intermediate
intermittent
interpret
interpretation
interrogate
interrupt
interview
intrigue
intrinsically
intuition

intuitive
invariably
inveigle
inveterate
involuntary
involvement
irascible
irrelevant
irreparable
irreplaceable
irresistible
irresponsible
irrevocable
irritable
italicize
itinerant
itinerary

J

jackal
jeopardize
jettisoned
jewellery
jodhpurs
juggernaut
jugular

K

kaleidoscopic
karate
keenness
khaki
kidnapped
kilometre
kiosk
kitchenette
kleptomania
knick-knack
knowledgeable
kowtow

L

labelled
laboratory
labyrinth
lackadaisical
laddered
lager
language
languor
languorous
laryngitis
larynx
lassitude

atitude
aundered
aunderette
ayette
eague
eanness
edger
egendary
egible
egitimate
ength
engthened
eukaemia
evelled
iaise
iaison
ieu
ieutenant
ilac
imousine
ineage
inen
ingerie
inguist
iqueur
literature
litre

livelihood
loneliness
loosened
loquacious
lorgnette
lucrative
lucre
luggage
lugubrious
luminous
luscious
lustre
luxurious
lyric

M

macabre
maelstrom
magician
magnanimous
mahogany
maintenance
malaise
malaria
malignant
manageable
management

mannequin
manoeuvre
mantelpiece
manually
margarine
marijuana
marquee
martyr
marvellous
marzipan
masochist
massacre
matinee
mayonnaise
meagre
measurement
medallion
medieval
mediocre
melancholy
meningitis
meringue
messenger
meteorological
metropolitan
microphone
midday

migraine
mileage
milieu
millionaire
mimicked
mimicry
miniature
miraculous
mirrored
miscellaneous
mischief
mischievous
misogynist
misshapen
misspell
misspent
modelled
modelling
morgue
mortgage
mosquito
mountaineer
moustache
multitudinous
museum
mysterious
mythical

N

naive
narrative
naughty
nausea
nautical
necessary
necessity
negligence
negligible
negotiate
neighbourhood
neither
neurotic
neutral
niche
niece
ninetieth
ninth
nocturnal
nonentity
notably
noticeably
notoriety
nuance
numbered
numerate

numerous
nutrient
nutritious

O

obedient
obese
obituary
oblige
oblique
oblivious
obnoxious
obscene
obscenity
obsessive
obstetrician
occasion
occupancy
occupier
occupying
occurred
occurrence
octogenarian
odorous
odour
offence
offered